Can you believe this?

Unbelievable Truths

That Are Stranger

Than Fiction

A Skill-Based Reading Anthology

Editorial Director: Susan C. Thies
Editor: Paula J. Reece
Writer: Janet Myers
Contributing Writer: Julie Cahalan
Book Design: Jann Williams
Production: Nancy Suits
Photo Research: Lisa Lorimor

Image Credits

© Roger Ressmeyer/CORBIS: 4; © AP, East Valley Tribune: 10; © AP, Journal Star: 19;
© AP: 26; © Greg Probst/CORBIS: 50; © Bettmann/CORBIS: 57;
© Richard T. Nowitz/CORBIS: 68; © Hulton-Deutsch Collection/CORBIS: 98

ArtToday: 77, 91, 107
Corbis: 115
Corel: 6–7, 44–45, 86–87
Dynamic Graphics: 8, 16, 24, 35, 46, 56, 65, 74, 88, 96, 104, 112
Eyewire: Cover
Library of Congress: 35

For information, contact
Perfection Learning® Corporation
1000 North Second Avenue, P.O. Box 500
Logan, Iowa 51546-0500.
Phone: 800-831-4190 • Fax: 800-543-2745
perfectionlearning.com

ISBN-10: 0-7891-5887-6 ISBN-13: 978-0-7891-5887-1
Printed in the U.S.A.
4 5 6 7 8 PP 12 11 10 09 08

contents

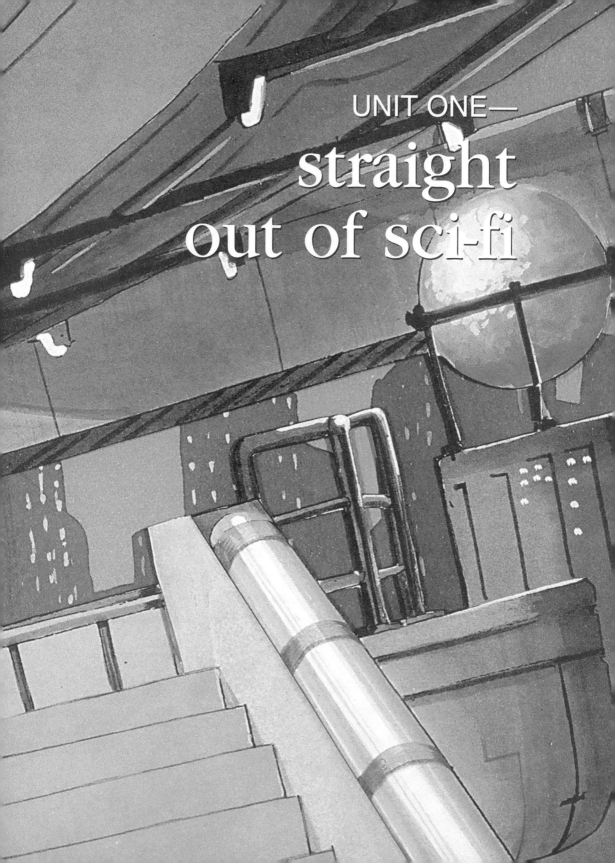

UNIT ONE—

straight out of sci-fi

Will Cryonics Work?

The deliberate freezing of a human body, after a "natural" death, might seem morbid. Why would anyone freeze a dead person?

[2]The following sounds like science fiction. But it really happened.

[3]Hospital doctors declared a man to be clinically dead. The man's family knew what to do. They asked that machines continue to keep blood and oxygen flowing in their relative's organs.

[4]A phone call was quickly made to a special emergency response team. Within hours, team members arrived and began to cool the man's body. They placed him in a special travel pack and rushed him to the airport.

[5]In an Arizona lab a few hours later, technicians pumped a glycerol-based solution into the man's veins. All of his blood was replaced. The solution worked like an anti-freeze. It reduced damage to cells. Next the body was slowly frozen over a 20-day period. Then the man's corpse was wrapped in aluminum foil. It was lowered into a large stainless steel cylinder. In the big container, liquid nitrogen further chilled the body to -320 degrees Fahrenheit.

[6]Years earlier, the man had arranged to be frozen after death. He now joined 30 other bodies in the cryonics storage area. It was a holding station for the future. Like his frozen companions, the man's goal was to preserve his body for many years. He hoped that at a future time, scientists would cure the disease that killed him and restore life to his preserved body.

[7]A crazy idea? Yes, according to most scientists. Skeptics say it's wishful dreaming and long-range planning. But it's not realistic.

[8]Cryonics, the freezing of bodies, began in 1967. That was the year the pioneer of the procedure was

frozen, or "suspended," as believers prefer. Dr. James Bedford was a 73-year-old retired psychology professor from California. Bedford made plans to be cryonically frozen shortly before he died from kidney cancer in January 1967.

[9]Bedford's cylinder made several moves to different storage areas, including two undignified trips in a U-Haul. Finally it ended up in Scottsdale, Arizona. Bedford rests in peace with other deep freeze "suspendees" in a cryonics foundation's warehouse.

[10]Cryonic suspension is expensive. And no one can guarantee that it will even work. A full-body suspension costs around $120,000. For less money, around $50,000, only a client's head is frozen. Yes, just the head. The theory here is that the person's preserved brain can someday be put into a new body.

[11]Four cryonics facilities exist, located in Michigan, California, and Arizona. Around 75 people are frozen and stored in the various locations. A few fans of cryonics had their pets frozen along with them. (Hopefully the pets got to die a natural death before becoming "petsicles"!) Around 800 more people are signed up to be cryonically suspended after they die.

[12]Biologists agree that it's easy to freeze people. The tricky part is thawing them out. Single cells, even small clusters of cells, have been frozen by scientists and then reanimated. But problems arise when large blocks of tissue are frozen. If many cells are frozen together, water between them expands. Spiky ice crystals form and rupture cell membranes. When this happens, damaged cells collapse.

[13]Some research does give hope. Frozen rat hearts have been cryo-preserved and then revived. But it's not clear if this would work for entire organisms, especially ones that are no longer living. No one can say for certain that science will ever be able to reanimate bodies. The people in cryonic suspension, however, are gambling that someday it will be possible.

[14]Supporters of cryonics are encouraged by present technology that preserves tissues. Human embryos, heart valves, corneas, and skin have all been reclaimed from ultra-low temperatures.

[15]So far, no entire brains have been frozen, then revived. Even if that happens, what about a person's memory and personality? Can they be preserved? Those who favor cryonics think so. They cite case

studies. For example, many people have nearly died in accidents when they were exposed to subzero temperatures. During some events, brain electrical activity stopped. But the individuals later had a total recovery.

[16]Cryonics believers claim that most brain structures can be preserved for a long period of time. They also feel that future scientists will know how to repair cell damage. Recent cell research does boost the hopes of cryonics cheerleaders. A big step has been taken toward growing new organs.

[17]Scientists conduct experiments with stem cells—the basic cells from which all of our human organs develop. While studying stem cells of mice, experimenters found out something important. Stem cells have the potential to become any type of tissue within the body, *if* they are given the correct genetic signals.

[18]A stumbling block here is that scientists haven't yet solved the *if*. They are unable to boot the switch to tell the cells which type of tissue to make. But the breakthrough is that stem cells are more flexible than was earlier thought. What does this mean for the future? One example is that new heart cells could be grown

Inside the Alcor Life Extension Foundation, a cryonics facility in Scottsdale, Arizona

to rebuild a person's diseased heart.

[19]Defenders of cryonics think that science of the future will be able to reverse the effects of aging. Believers dream of living again, cured of whatever disease killed them.

[20]Nonbelievers say "hogwash!" A

dead body is a dead body, they declare. It will never be renewed after cryo-freezing. Cell damage that occurs when one dies can't be reversed. They also challenge the idea that a person's mind and personality could be preserved in a frozen brain.

[21]Cryonics can't be called a booming business, but backers insist that someday it'll be more widely accepted. Future growth is expected as researchers succeed in freezing and thawing undamaged organs. More people will then be interested in cryonic suspension.

[22]Critics say it will never be accepted as anything but a fad for a few people grasping to live forever. Doubters mock the idea that death can be cheated in a deep-freeze limbo. They label cryonics as a quack science. The scientists say cryonics societies are turning gullible people into expensive "freezer pops."

[23]Then there are the religious questions attacking cryonics. What happens to the frozen person's soul? Religious ethics suggest lots of complications.

[24]Controversial subjects like cryonics have no easy answers. During struggles to study facts, logic often scuffles with emotions. Debates will continue: Is it moral? Is it sensible?

[25]Would you want your body frozen? Yes or no—either way, it's an intriguing subject to think about.

If you have been timing your reading speed for this story, record your time below.

_____ : _____

Minutes   ***Seconds***

UNDERSTANDING THE MAIN IDEA

The following questions will demonstrate your understanding of what the story is about, or the *main idea*. Choose the best answer for each question.

1. This story is mainly about

Ⓐ people who donate their organs for scientific research.

Ⓑ stem cell research.

Ⓒ people who are frozen at death, hoping they'll be brought back to life.

Ⓓ the growth of cancer cells.

2. This story could have been titled

Ⓐ "The Future of Cells."

Ⓑ "The Hope for a Continued Life."

Ⓒ "Pets—Loyal Beyond Life."

Ⓓ "Brain Transplants."

3. Which detail best supports the main idea of the story?

Ⓐ Scientists conduct experiments with stem cells.

Ⓑ Dr. James Bedford was a 73-year-old retired psychology professor from California.

Ⓒ Many people have nearly died in accidents when they were exposed to subzero temperatures.

Ⓓ The man hoped that future scientists would cure the disease that killed him and restore life to his frozen body.

4. Find another detail that supports the main idea of this story. Write it on the lines below.

_____

_____

RECALLING FACTS

The following questions will test how well you remember the facts in the story you just read. Choose the best answer for each question.

1. The man's body was chilled to

Ⓐ -320 degrees Fahrenheit.

Ⓑ -32 degrees Fahrenheit.

Ⓒ 32 degrees Fahrenheit.

Ⓓ 0 degrees Fahrenheit.

2. Cryonics is

Ⓐ the curing of disease.

Ⓑ the removal of frozen bodies.

Ⓒ the freezing of bodies or body parts.

Ⓓ bringing a brain back to life in a new body.

3. Single cells have been frozen by scientists, but

Ⓐ it's difficult to freeze large blocks of tissue.

Ⓑ the cells had to be thrown away.

Ⓒ most turned to water when thawed.

Ⓓ it's hard to reanimate larger tissues.

4. Present technology has not been able to reclaim

Ⓐ embryos from very low temperatures.

Ⓑ brains from very low temperatures.

Ⓒ corneas from very low temperatures.

Ⓓ skin from very low temperatures.

———— ■ ————

Can You Believe This?

READING BETWEEN THE LINES

An *inference* is a conclusion drawn from facts. A *generalization* is a general statement, idea, or rule that is supported by facts. Analyze the story by choosing the best answer to each question below.

1. What conclusion can you draw from paragraphs 4–5?

ⓐ The doctors wanted to perform research on the man's body.

ⓑ The team wanted to bring the man back to life in the next week.

ⓒ There are several predetermined steps to freezing a body.

ⓓ The man died in Arizona.

2. What conclusion can you draw from paragraphs 12–13?

ⓐ Scientists have been experimenting with freezing cells and tissues.

ⓑ Cryonics has no scientific support.

ⓒ Freezing an entire human body will always be a scientific impossibility.

ⓓ There is no place to keep thousands of frozen bodies.

3. What generalization can you make from the story?

ⓐ Some scientific theories continue to be debated.

ⓑ Cryonics will never work with humans.

ⓒ Most supporters of cryonics die of cancer.

ⓓ No one believes cryonics will really work.

4. It can be inferred from the story that

ⓐ almost everyone is willing to try cryonics.

ⓑ a person must be clinically dead to be frozen.

ⓒ cryonics has almost no supporters.

ⓓ there is no scientific evidence that frozen tissue can be brought back to life.

DETERMINING CAUSE AND EFFECT

Choose the best answers for the following questions to show the relationship between what happened in the story (*effects*) and why those things happened (*causes*).

1. Because some people hope to return to life after death, they

  Ⓐ are asking to be reawakened with electricity.

  Ⓑ are considered insane and their wishes are ignored.

  Ⓒ request to be frozen until science can revive them.

  Ⓓ commit suicide before they die of natural causes.

2. What happens because some people think a preserved brain will be able to be placed in a new body?

  Ⓐ They are having just their heads frozen.

  Ⓑ They are trying to create robotic bodies.

  Ⓒ They are saving up money to pay for future medical advancements.

  Ⓓ They know it costs less than having their entire bodies preserved.

3. Why do cryonics supporters think memory and personality can be preserved in a frozen body?

  Ⓐ It's a well-known scientific fact.

  Ⓑ Scientific research has proven it recently.

  Ⓒ Rats' brains have been frozen and then reawakened with no loss of personality or memory.

  Ⓓ Individuals who have been exposed to freezing temperatures have had total recoveries.

4. Why do cryonics critics think that the process will never work? Write two reasons given in the selection on the lines below, using complete sentences.

_____

_____

_____

_____

_____

_____

—————— ■ ——————

Can You Believe This?

USING CONTEXT CLUES

Skilled readers often find the meaning of unfamiliar words by using *context clues*. This means they study the way the words are used in the text. Use the context clues in the excerpts below to determine the meaning of each **bold-faced** word. Then choose the answer that best matches the meaning of the word.

1. "Like his frozen **companions**, the man's goal was to preserve his body for many years."

CLUE: "[He] now joined 30 other bodies in the cryonics storage area."

   Ⓐ companies

   Ⓑ pets

   Ⓒ fellows

   Ⓓ fighters

2. "Four cryonics **facilities** exist, located in Michigan, California, and Arizona."

CLUE: "Around 75 people are frozen and stored in the various locations."

   Ⓐ arguments

   Ⓑ scientists

   Ⓒ uses

   Ⓓ buildings

3. "Single cells, even small clusters of cells, have been frozen by scientists and then **reanimated**."

CLUE: "Frozen rat hearts have been cryo-preserved and then revived."

   Ⓐ broken down

   Ⓑ brought back to life

   Ⓒ drawn again

   Ⓓ temporarily prevented from functioning

4. "But the breakthrough is that stem cells are more **flexible** than was earlier thought."

CLUE: "Stem cells have the potential to become any type of tissue within the body, *if* they are given the correct genetic signals."

   Ⓐ adaptable

   Ⓑ bendable

   Ⓒ deadly

   Ⓓ confusing

Are Crop Circles a Hoax?

The farmer felt a chill run down his back. He knew something had happened. He sensed it, but he saw nothing unusual. Climbing a small hill, the man looked down on his sea of golden wheat.

[2] Yes, there it was. Flattened wheat stalks formed two huge circles joined by straight lines. Small outer circles completed the pattern pressed into the wheat field.

[3] The farmer knew mysterious crop circles had appeared in neighboring fields. But it was different seeing one on his own land. Scary, yet exciting.

[4] How did these circles and lines get here? Aliens did it, said some people. UFOs (Unidentified Flying Objects) were accused of swirling the grain when they landed in these fields of southern England. Starting in the mid-1960s, strange lights sometimes flashed in the local night skies, boosting the UFO theory.

[5] The farmer turned toward his house. He decided to make a phone call to report this incident. Soon others would notice the crop circles.

Curious thrill seekers and reporters would swarm to the field.

[6] Hundreds of crop circles have dotted the English countryside since the early 1980s. And similar formations emerged in other countries around the world. The grain fields of southern England, however, have hosted most of the appearances.

[7] Like magic, crop circles appear in fields overnight. Each circle ranges in size from 10 feet to over 100 feet in diameter. Besides circles, the designs include ringed circles, lines, wheels with spokes, triangles, and rectangles. The backdrop for the artwork can be various types of grain but is commonly wheat, oats, or barley.

[8] Self-styled experts studied the crop circles. They noticed that the plants were pressed hard to the ground and usually swirled clockwise. Grain stems were bent but not broken. The flattened stalks

16

were still alive.

[9]The cause of crop circles baffled everyone, but people offered lots of guesses. Natural forces were to blame, according to some people. The formations could be the result of windstorms, lightning, or static electricity.

[10]Another possible culprit was the weather. A meteorologist suggested a "plasma vortex" theory. He described spinning columns of positive-charged air. The whirlwinds rush across the hills and twist grain stalks into the different shapes.

[11]Animals were also blamed. One circle solver blamed culprits such as troops of crazed badgers running around in circles.

[12]An even more dramatic viewpoint was proposed by UFO buffs. They claimed the patterns represent coded messages from outer space visitors.

[13]Weird lights in the night skies and suddenly visible crop circles were not the only creepy things in the English countryside. Humminglike noises were reported. Sometimes crackling electrical sounds zapped through the air. Eerie knocking noises were heard in the region.

[14]In the 1980s the circles attracted followers of what has been called the New Age Movement. New Agers believed the circles had supernatural powers or spiritual meanings. Magnetic disturbances were noted. Spiritual leaders conducted seances, putting themselves in trances while sitting within the crop circles. Cosmic energy was credited for the special forces.

[15]One fact stood out. No one had ever witnessed a crop circle being formed. One group wanted to be the first to do so. In June of 1989 a "cropwatch" was held near a valley called the Punchbowl—a site of dozens of formations. For one week video cameras ran day and night. Volunteers watched video monitors and kept weather logs of the temperature, barometric pressure, and wind direction. Nothing happened. Nothing at all.

[16]By 1990 circles were "cropping up" in other areas of England, as well as in other countries. Patterns grew more complex. Pictograms emerged in shapes like stars, animals, and letters of the alphabet. Hoaxes were suspected.

[17]In July 1990, an enormous and elaborate pattern appeared. Dozens of satellite circles surrounded large ringed circles. So many sightseers came to gawk that the farmer who owned the field charged entrance fees.

[18]A year later in the summer of 1991, circle fans were stunned. Two men confessed.

[19]Doug Brewer and Dave Chorley admitted they'd been making crop circles for over ten years. Both were ordinary working-class men now in their sixties.

[20]They complained that others began copying them—more and more pranksters each year. But Doug and Dave claimed to be the original tricksters. They wanted recognition for being able to pull off their secret stunts for so many years.

[21]The men revealed how they had sketched samples on napkins or paper then picked a design-of-the-night. Doug and Dave laughed at the publicity earned by their grainfield creations. The two friends especially chuckled at one newspaper article. It quoted a circle expert who gushed praise for one of their random patterns. The expert said the geometric design showed superior mathematical ability—possibly made by beings from another planet.

[22]Why did Doug and Dave make crop circles? "Just for fun," explained Dave. Their nighttime antics usually had followed a stopover in a local pub. Now the men were getting older and ready to retire from their tricks. They were willing to share their secrets.

[23]How did they do it? Mainly with foot power. According to Doug and Dave, this is the way you make a crop circle:

[24]The tools are simple. You need a 4-foot-long wooden plank with a rope tied to each end. Hold the ropes and place the plank beneath one foot. Walking upright, step down to bend grain stalks with each step. Also hold tight to a string tied to a central pole. This keeps you walking in a circle.

[25]Like Doug, wear a baseball cap. On the bill of the cap, attach a wire that hangs in front of your face. Dangling from the short wire is a metal ring. You can stalk-stomp in a straight line by using one eye to peer through the ring. You sight (through the ring) a distant light or a faint object and walk straight toward it.

[26](Although Doug and Dave did not mention this, it should be noted that farmers do not like people trampling through their grainfields. Therefore, this is not an *advisable hobby*.)

[27]After the confession of the two men, several pranksters came forward and admitted trying to outdo Doug and Dave's artwork.

[28]However, the party was not over. In 1992 a hoax contest held in

Can You Believe This?

England brought together groups of enthusiastic circle makers. The gleeful contestants crushed, pressed, and stomped the grainfields into fancy formations. Onlookers were wowed by the artistic skills of the gung-ho competitors.

[29] You might think this ended the crop circle mystery. Most people simply wrote off crop circles as the shenanigans of Doug, Dave, and their copycats. Not everyone was satisfied, though.

[30] Diehards insist that pranksters are not totally responsible. The confession of Doug and Dave is called a "hoaxed hoax." Crop circle supporters refuse to credit the two men and others with all the formations. Defenders stick to the opinion that some of the circles were not made by humans. For them, the mystery continues.

[31] It's argued that physical evidence backs up these believers. A scientist closely examined a circle thought to be authentic. According to the scientist, the cell structures of the plants were malformed in peculiar ways. He was unable to suggest how these changes occurred.

[32] Some defenders point out that mysteriously made crop circles are not just a recent happening. Oddly, crop circles do have an older history.

[33] Way back in 1678, a document recorded an event declared to be the work of Satan. In this same area of southern England, circular patches of wheat were cut by an unknown creature. The early crop circle maker was called the "Mowing Devil."

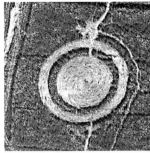

A mysterious crop circle appeared in a barley field near Lincoln, Nebraska.

[34] Circles were also mentioned in a book written 300 years ago by an Oxford University professor. He wondered what they were. The professor decided the patterns were made either by animals or by lightning.

[35] So if crop circle reports have been around for such a long time, questions remain. Are all the circles that appeared over the years the work of hoaxers? Or are some circles genuine—the result of still unexplained events? What do you think?

If you have been timing your reading speed for this story, record your time below.

_____ : _____

Minutes   Seconds

UNDERSTANDING THE MAIN IDEA

The following questions will demonstrate your understanding of what the story is about, or the *main idea*. Choose the best answer for each question.

1. This story is mainly about

Ⓐ the rotation of different kinds of crops in one field.

Ⓑ mysterious designs left in crop fields.

Ⓒ the funniest hoaxes in British folklore.

Ⓓ an unproven story of farmers who trade land.

2. This story could have been titled

Ⓐ "Trading Crops with Your Neighbors."

Ⓑ "Extraterrestrial Activities in Australia."

Ⓒ "The Truth About Crop Circles."

Ⓓ "One Farmer's False Claim to Fame."

3. Which detail best supports the main idea of the story?

Ⓐ Starting in the mid-1960s, strange lights sometimes flashed in the local night skies.

Ⓑ Like magic, crop circles appeared in fields overnight.

Ⓒ Grain stems were bent but not broken.

Ⓓ Magnetic disturbances were noted in the crop circles.

4. Find another detail that supports the main idea of this story. Write it on the lines below.

_____

_____

RECALLING FACTS

The following questions will test how well you remember the facts in the story you just read. Choose the best answer for each question.

1. Name three things people blamed crop circles on. Answer on the lines below, using complete sentences.

_____

_____

_____

_____

_____

2. Most crop circles have appeared in

Ⓐ southern England.

Ⓑ Northern Ireland.

Ⓒ the Midwest of the United States.

Ⓓ western Australia.

3. Two men said they had

Ⓐ found the aliens that made crop circles.

Ⓑ figured out the weather phenomena that caused the patterns.

Ⓒ discovered that the patterns were really a map.

Ⓓ made the crop circles as a prank.

4. Crop circles have a history dating back to the

Ⓐ 800s.

Ⓑ 1400s.

Ⓒ 1600s.

Ⓓ 1990s.

Can You Believe This?

READING BETWEEN THE LINES

An *inference* is a conclusion drawn from facts. A *generalization* is a general statement, idea, or rule that is supported by facts. Analyze the story by choosing the best answer to each question below.

1. What conclusion can you draw from paragraphs 1–5?

Ⓐ The farmer knew how the patterns in his field had been made.

Ⓑ The farmer was hoping scientists would find the aliens who had destroyed his fields.

Ⓒ The farmer thought this was the first time this had ever happened.

Ⓓ The farmer wanted people to come look at his fields.

2. What conclusion can you draw from paragraphs 21–22?

Ⓐ Doug and Dave felt that spirits were telling them what to draw in the fields.

Ⓑ Doug and Dave felt the crop circles were harmless fun.

Ⓒ The pub owner knew all along who was making the designs.

Ⓓ It was hard for Doug and Dave to decide on designs.

3. What generalization can you make from the story?

Ⓐ No one thought two men could make the designs.

Ⓑ Everyone believed Doug and Dave.

Ⓒ Many people believe the crop circles have now been explained.

Ⓓ Most farmers were excited when designs appeared in their fields.

4. It can be inferred from the story that

Ⓐ Doug and Dave had their friends help them make circles.

Ⓑ Doug and Dave didn't really make any of the circles.

Ⓒ Doug and Dave couldn't have made all the designs.

Ⓓ Doug and Dave were once known as the "Mowing Devil."

Can You Believe This?

DETERMINING CAUSE AND EFFECT

Choose the best answers for the following questions to show the relationship between what happened in the story (*effects*) and why those things happened (*causes*).

1. Because no one really knew what caused the crop circles,

Ⓐ farmers stopped planting again until the circles stopped appearing.

Ⓑ many people offered their guesses as to what was causing them.

Ⓒ anyone caught in someone else's field was arrested.

Ⓓ scientists tried to re-create the crop circles in test fields.

2. What happened because no one had ever seen a crop circle being formed?

Ⓐ Many people denied that crop circles existed at all.

Ⓑ Volunteers videotaped a field for a week to try to catch the makers.

Ⓒ It was widely believed that the makers were invisible.

Ⓓ The farmers charged admission to view the designs.

3. Why did several people come forward after Doug and Dave confessed?

Ⓐ They were upset that Doug and Dave were trying to claim the hoax they'd created.

Ⓑ They knew Doug and Dave hadn't made any of the designs.

Ⓒ They admitted that they were trying to outdo Doug and Dave.

Ⓓ They had helped Doug and Dave design the patterns.

4. Why did some believers in the crop circle mystery say that crop circles were not just a recent happening?

Ⓐ They were lying to support their theories that aliens had created the circles.

Ⓑ They proved a connection between crop circles and circles of standing stones.

Ⓒ They knew wind had been making the circles for centuries.

Ⓓ Two 300-year-old documents mentioned similar occurrences.

USING CONTEXT CLUES

Skilled readers often find the meaning of unfamiliar words by using *context clues*. This means they study the way the words are used in the text. Use the context clues in the excerpts below to determine the meaning of each **bold-faced** word. Then choose the answer that best matches the meaning of the word.

1. "He [The farmer] decided to make a phone call to report this **incident**."

CLUE: "He knew something had happened. . . . Flattened wheat stalks formed two huge circles joined by straight lines."

    Ⓐ crime

    Ⓑ parade

    Ⓒ happening

    Ⓓ weather

2. "Another possible **culprit** [for the crop circles] was the weather."

CLUE: "The formations could be the result of windstorms, lightning, or static electricity."

    Ⓐ cause

    Ⓑ result

    Ⓒ person

    Ⓓ criminal

3. "In July 1990, an enormous and **elaborate** pattern appeared."

CLUE: "Dozens of satellite circles surrounded large ringed circles."

    Ⓐ simple

    Ⓑ small

    Ⓒ happy

    Ⓓ complicated

4. "Doug and Dave laughed at the **publicity** earned by their grainfield creations."

CLUE: "The two friends especially chuckled at one newspaper article."

    Ⓐ money

    Ⓑ attention

    Ⓒ schooling

    Ⓓ public

What Are Wormholes in Space?

W^{hen} our planet Earth is described as just a speck in the universe, it's not an exaggeration. The vastness of space is absolutely mind-boggling.

[2] Our solar system, the sun and nine planets, seems big to us. But it represents only a tiny spot in our huge Milky Way galaxy. Crossing the Milky Way, with its billions of stars, would take us 100,000 light-years. That is, *if* we could zoom at the speed of light, at about 186,000 miles per second. We have a long way to go to travel that fast. Right now, our astronauts reach a top speed of a measly 7 miles per second.

[3] Our spiral-shaped Milky Way is a member of a clump of galaxies known as the Local Group. The Local Group belongs to a Local Supercluster of galaxies that spreads nearly 100 million light-years across. Stretching beyond this are millions of other galaxies. Feeling small yet?

[4] Many years into the future, maybe humans will learn how to travel close to the speed of light. In one light-year, a spaceship would zip through 6 trillion miles of space. However, our neighbor spiral galaxy, the Andromeda, is more than a whopping 2 million light-years away. Can we hope to ever explore the cosmos that spans such endless distances? One idea is to use cryonics—freeze astronauts' bodies and revive them when they arrive at their destination. But we can't be certain that cryonics will work. Are there other choices for long space journeys?

[5] What if we discover shortcuts? Some scientists believe that wormholes may be the answer. Just as a worm burrows through an apple as a shortcut from one side to the other, a wormhole in space connects two widely separated regions in space. Could humans

voyage to faraway locations in the universe by way of wormholes?

[6]This sounds like a scene from a *Star Trek* movie. But 100 years ago, our everyday gadgets and events of today would have seemed like science fiction—television, computers, jets, men walking on the moon, and cell phones. So think ahead 600 years. Maybe you are an ancestor of people who will use "gateways" to visit colonies in outer space. Where will they find these gateways? Let's go back a few years.

[7]In the early 1900s, our understanding of the mysterious universe got a boost from an unknown genius named Albert Einstein. He stunned the scientific world. He shook the foundations of physics with his astonishing concepts. Physics is the science dealing with matter and energy and how they interact with each other.

[8]Einstein's Special Theory of Relativity explained that all time is relative. For example, time slows down for objects traveling at incredible speeds near the speed of light. A spaceship moving this swiftly could be gone from Earth one year, according to the onboard clock. When the space travelers return, at the end of their one year, 223 years would have passed on Earth.

[9]More new ways of thinking began when Einstein next presented a General Theory of Relativity. He showed that gravity, space, and time are linked in the universe. Space has the three familiar dimensions of height, width, and depth. Plus, it has an extra dimension of space-time. This is because all objects in space are moving and are located in time as well as in space. Gravity warps space-time. So space is distorted, or curved, by the matter and energy in it.

[10]For the rest of the century, Einstein's numerous fresh ideas helped scientists tackle puzzles of the universe. One of the strangest things they studied was black holes. Massive collapsed stars with runaway gravity were likely candidates to become black holes. Even though astronomers couldn't see these oddities, they knew black holes existed because of how they affected their surroundings.

[11]Think of a black hole as a cosmic funnel. Inside, the gravity is so powerful that nothing escapes— not even light. Anything pulled into a black hole cannot get back out. But here's the really weird part. Deep in the well of a black hole is the singularity. This is the point where gravity is so super-strong that all matter simply vanishes. All time,

space, matter, and energy end here.

[12]Where does it all go?

[13]Scientists can only guess. Some suggest that the singularity is a tunnel, or wormhole, leading to a white hole. The white hole is like a reverse-image of a black hole. Whatever a black hole swallows, a white hole spits out. The white hole is an exit that leaps across enormous distances of curved space.

[14]Another theory is that the white hole connects to an entirely different universe. Truth and fiction seem entangled. No wonder science fiction writers are fond of weaving black holes and white holes into their stories.

[15]Physicists agree that an astronaut would not like the assignment of exploring a black hole. Imagine a person in a spacesuit entering a black hole, feet first. Gravity pulls harder on the astronaut's lower body and "spaghettifies" the person, stretching him or her into a piece of spaghetti. As if that's not enough, the astronaut's body probably explodes when it invades the unimaginable forces of the singularity.

[16]Can black holes be tamed so that humans could survive and travel through a wormhole? Besides overcoming the frenzy of the

Carl Sagan

singularity, there's another problem. The tunnel itself would collapse on anything trying to pass through it. Maybe future scientists can invent what is called *exotic material*. This would be some type of anti-gravity substance. The idea is to reinforce the wormhole—prop it open by counteracting the extreme gravity. Two-way traffic can then take place through the stable wormhole tunnel. A person could both enter and leave. All of this is the kind of thinking scientists throw back and forth as a "what-if" possibility.

[17]Serious thought was given to wormholes in the mid-1980s. Writer-astronomer Carl Sagan was working on a novel called *Contact*. He wanted to be as realistic as possible when his characters zipped through the cosmos. Sagan approached California Institute of Technology's Kip Thorne, asking for a solution to an interstellar voyage. Thorne

proposed that Sagan's characters use a wormhole. He also described its design and how it could work.

[18]Other scientists agree with Thorne that wormholes might someday be used for space travel. However, the solutions must be achieved by a future society that is much more advanced than we are now.

[19]Suppose we could journey back to the past or visit the future. Fantasy? Perhaps not. It was suggested that wormholes might lead to time travel. Stephen Hawking, one of the most respected physicists of recent years, disagreed. He concluded that the laws of physics do not allow time travel. Hawking summed up the debate by saying, "The best evidence we have that time travel is not possible, and never will be, is that we have not been invaded by hordes of visitors from the future."

[20]Topics like wormholes in space are far-fetched to some scientists.

Others, though, gush with excitement when picturing wormholes as deep-space gateways. Occasionally they even use science fiction-sounding terms like "gravity shield" and "warp drive."

[21]Since the 1990s, the Hubble Space Telescope has allowed us to peek at space's limitless borders. Skeptics claim that humans will never conquer travel throughout the overwhelming universe. That challenge will motivate others to probe secrets that turn starship dreams into reality.

[22]On a clear night, gaze skyward at the canopy of stars against an inky velvet background. It's easy to feel small when facing the glittering spectacle. But remember that we live in a thrilling time. Ongoing scientific discoveries will point future generations toward gateways to the universe. In our lifetime, we might be granted a glimpse at wonders yet to come.

If you have been timing your reading speed for this story, record your time below.

_____ : _____

Minutes   **Seconds**

UNDERSTANDING THE MAIN IDEA

The following questions will demonstrate your understanding of what the story is about, or the *main idea*. Choose the best answer for each question.

1. This story is mainly about

Ⓐ ways to travel to the future.

Ⓑ the way the Milky Way galaxy formed.

Ⓒ possible "shortcuts" for space travel.

Ⓓ the way gravity affects hollow objects in space.

2. This story could have been titled

Ⓐ "Tunnels for Space Travel."

Ⓑ "Making Contact with Other Galaxies."

Ⓒ "Not Just Black and White."

Ⓓ "All About Gravity."

3. Which detail best supports the main idea of the story?

Ⓐ Our everyday gadgets and way of life would have been called science fiction 100 years ago.

Ⓑ Physics is the science dealing with matter and energy and how they interact with one another.

Ⓒ Some scientists think a black hole's center is a tunnel to a white hole.

Ⓓ Carl Sagan was working on a science fiction novel called *Contact*.

4. Find another detail that supports the main idea of this story. Write it on the lines below.

_____

_____

RECALLING FACTS

The following questions will test how well you remember the facts in the story you just read. Choose the best answer for each question.

1. The Milky Way belongs to a group of galaxies called

Ⓐ Mega G.

Ⓑ the Local Group.

Ⓒ M&M/Mars.

Ⓓ Alpha Omega.

2. A wormhole is thought to be

Ⓐ a shortcut through huge space distances.

Ⓑ the opposite of a meteor.

Ⓒ the oldest form of planets.

Ⓓ the quickest way to Mars.

3. Albert Einstein's Special Theory of Relativity explained that all time is

Ⓐ wasted.

Ⓑ imaginary.

Ⓒ relative.

Ⓓ valuable.

4. Black holes could come from

Ⓐ large collapsed stars.

Ⓑ large meteors hurtling through space.

Ⓒ space shuttles that upset the balance of the universe.

Ⓓ collisions between two rapidly moving galaxies.

Can You Believe This?

READING BETWEEN THE LINES

An *inference* is a conclusion drawn from facts. A *generalization* is a general statement, idea, or rule that is supported by facts. Analyze the story by choosing the best answer to each question below.

1. What conclusion can you draw from paragraphs 11–13?

Ⓐ Matter in black holes evaporates and doesn't really "go" anywhere.

Ⓑ Scientists aren't sure where matter that disappears in a black hole goes.

Ⓒ Black holes don't really exist.

Ⓓ Scientist haven't correctly interpreted Einstein's theories.

2. What conclusion can you draw from paragraph 15?

Ⓐ An astronaut would die going into a black hole.

Ⓑ Humans have the ability, but not the courage, to go through wormholes.

Ⓒ Those who have traveled through black holes have found it very painful.

Ⓓ Going through a wormhole causes a time warp.

3. What generalization can you make from the story?

Ⓐ Most scientists are confident that wormholes will allow time travel.

Ⓑ All science fiction stories include black holes.

Ⓒ No one will ever figure out how to travel through space.

Ⓓ Future generations will be more likely to participate in space-time travel.

4. It can be inferred from the story that

Ⓐ there is very much about space that we don't yet know.

Ⓑ humans will soon be traveling millions of light-years away.

Ⓒ science fiction stories have no connection to science.

Ⓓ we will never know what a black hole really is.

Can You Believe This?

DETERMINING CAUSE AND EFFECT

Choose the best answers for the following questions to show the relationship between what happened in the story (*effects*) and why those things happened (*causes*).

1. Because gravity warps space-time,

Ⓐ people living on the moon don't age.

Ⓑ space is curved by the matter and energy it holds.

Ⓒ it's easy to bounce between galaxies.

Ⓓ there is no way to measure a true light-year.

2. What happened because Einstein came up with fresh ideas about gravity, space, and time?

Ⓐ He was expelled from Germany.

Ⓑ Scientists started looking at space questions in a new way.

Ⓒ He was not allowed to join the Royal Order of Astronomers.

Ⓓ No one took his ideas seriously until a telescope could prove them.

3. Why is there nothing inside a black hole?

Ⓐ Gravity is so powerful that all matter vanishes.

Ⓑ A force field surrounding it makes everything bounce back into space.

Ⓒ It's against international law to place satellites in black holes.

Ⓓ A new star is developing there.

4. Why isn't time travel possible, according to Stephen Hawking?

Ⓐ He hasn't been able to do it.

Ⓑ Laws of physics don't allow time travel.

Ⓒ Earth's gravity is too strong.

Ⓓ The Hubble Space Telescope has proven humans can't travel to the past.

Can You Believe This?

USING CONTEXT CLUES

Skilled readers often find the meaning of unfamiliar words by using *context clues*. This means they study the way the words are used in the text. Use the context clues in the excerpts below to determine the meaning of each **bold-faced** word. Then choose the answer that best matches the meaning of the word.

1. "Can we hope to ever explore the **cosmos** that spans such endless distances?"

CLUE: "In one light-year a spaceship would zip through 6 trillion miles of space. . . . [Andromeda] is more than a whopping 2 million light-years away."

   Ⓐ highway

   Ⓑ space

   Ⓒ bridge

   Ⓓ distance

2. "He [Albert Einstein] stunned the scientific world. He shook the foundations of physics with his astonishing **concepts**."

CLUE: "For the rest of the century, Einstein's numerous fresh ideas helped scientists tackle puzzles of the universe."

   Ⓐ ideas

   Ⓑ clothes

   Ⓒ strength

   Ⓓ attitude

3. "Gravity **warps** space-time."

CLUE: "So space is distorted, or curved, by the matter and energy in it."

   Ⓐ speeds up

   Ⓑ slows down

   Ⓒ straightens

   Ⓓ bends

4. "On a clear night, gaze skyward at the **canopy** of stars against an inky velvet background." (paragraph 22)

Write what you think the **bold-faced** word means. Then record the context clues that led you to this definition.

Meaning:

_____

_____

_____

Context clues:

_____

_____

_____

—— ▬ ——

Who Believes in Haunted Houses?

Several years ago a young couple named Jason and Kate did an impulsive thing. They accepted a challenge to spend a night in a "haunted" house.

[2] Like haunted houses across the country, this one was supposed to be inhabited by ghosts. The massive three-story structure had stood deserted for years. Once an elegant residence, it now sagged under a gloomy shroud of abandonment. Years ago the house silently observed violence. Three people were tortured and killed before the deranged murderer committed suicide. Tales of horror, retold over the years, gave the dwelling local fame as a place to avoid.

[3] The last family who attempted to reside in the house left within a week. Each night they were startled by noises. Knocking sounds echoed throughout. Eerie music played from the empty attic. Doors slammed. From vacant rooms came murmuring voices, sometimes changing to mournful sobs.

[4] One night, sensing that someone was in the hallway, the father of the family arose from bed. He peeked into the hallway from his bedroom doorway. Flicking on the light, he glimpsed a woman in a flowing gown hurrying around the corner toward the staircase. The man darted after the intruder. To his astonishment, the mysterious woman had vanished. A nearby mocking laugh caused a chill to creep up the man's arms. Enough was enough. The next day the terrorized family moved out.

[5] So why did Jason and Kate agree to spend a night in such a spooky place? For money, of course.

[6] A local newspaper owner had recently bought the property. Soon the old house would be torn down to make way for the newspaper's

office building. A writer suggested an idea for a story—offer a nice reward for any couple who would stay overnight in the haunted house. Afterward, the writer would interview the volunteers for a newspaper story about the experience.

[7]The selected couple was Jason and Kate. They did not believe in ghosts, but Jason and Kate did believe in nice rewards. They eagerly accepted the dare.

[8]Now here they were, toting backpacks and sleeping bags, about to enter the dark, musty-smelling house. A short distance away, security guards were posted to prevent pranksters from hassling the couple and to verify that Jason and Kate stayed inside all night. Other than that, the pair was on their own. Rules were simple. They had to stay in the house from 10 p.m. until 8 a.m. Spend ten hours inside the haunted house, and earn big money. Easy enough—so they thought.

[9]Jason unlocked the creaking door. They stepped into a large, round two-story foyer. On the left, a rickety winding staircase led to the second floor. Their flashlights pierced the darkness to reveal the cobwebs and dinginess of their run-down overnight shelter. It didn't look *too* bad.

[10]Kate placed several lit candles around the big entryway. With a steady stream of cheerful chatter, they unrolled sleeping bags. They'd camp right there, near the front door. There was no reason to venture into any other rooms. People at the newspaper office promised that no tricks would be involved. Jason and Kate were guaranteed of being left completely alone.

[11]As planned, they prepared to go directly to sleep—an easy way to spend the required ten hours. One big candle was left burning. Their talking turned to whispers that soon trailed off into silence. Surprisingly, both fell asleep quickly.

[12]All at once, Jason awoke with a start. He sat straight up. What was the sound that had stirred him? Then he realized where he was. It was totally dark in the room.

[13]"Kate, are you awake?"

[14]"Yes," Kate answered in a tense whisper. "Did you hear that loud shriek? And I think I heard footsteps—and a person crying. What happened to our candle?"

[15]Jason groped in the darkness for a box of matches. As he struck a match, he was aware of a sudden coldness in the room. His hand trembled. Jason relit the candle and looked into Kate's frightened face.

He followed her wide-eyed stare to a sudden movement at the top of the stairs. Someone, or something, had just scurried out of sight.

[16]Although Jason's nervous voice betrayed him, he reassured Kate that the disturbance was probably some kind of animal living in the house.

[17]It was only about 2 a.m. The two talked in low voices, trying to think of jokes—anything to take their minds off the subject of where they were. It didn't work.

[18]During a long pause, they heard faint music that was shrill and creepy. It stopped. The couple listened hard. A tapping came from someplace upstairs, accompanied by a muffled moan. In the candlelight Kate's pale face reflected Jason's own rising anxiety. The moaning sound grew louder. Jason felt the hair on the back of his neck tingle. Their candle went out.

[19]Jason's shaky hands spilled the box of matches. Finally, he lit a match. It flickered briefly until a sudden breeze extinguished the flame. Jason grabbed a flashlight and quickly scanned the shadowy round room. Nothing. But he sensed that eyes were watching them.

[20]Needless to say, Jason and Kate didn't last the ten hours. More noises convinced them that they'd had

enough. Someone else could try for the reward. This was a scarier ordeal than expected.

[21]Did Jason and Kate give up too quickly? Had they merely frightened themselves with overactive imaginations? Are there such things as haunted houses?

[22]Each state in our country has dozens of dwellings with a reputation of being haunted. These houses have colorful pasts that make them part of local folklore. They also have other things in common.

[23]*Usually tragedy or violence has occurred inside the houses. This ranges from fatal illnesses to bloody murders.*

[24]One such house is the Octagon in Washington, D.C.

[25]The Octagon has had several different owners during its turbulent history. Both daughters of an early owner died tragically. The older daughter fell over the stairway's second-floor railing, crashing to the marble floor below. Soon the second daughter met her death, tumbling down the same steep staircase.

[26]A later owner heard thumping sounds from a wall. He had workmen break it open. Stuffed inside the wall was the skeleton of an anonymous woman. After she was properly buried, the thumps stopped.

Can You Believe This?

[27]On another occasion, a gambler was shot to death in the house by a man he'd cheated. Shortly afterward, during the Civil War, the Octagon was used as a hospital for soldiers. And it was a hideout for runaway slaves.

[28]By the late 1800s, several people had reported seeing ghosts or hearing sobs and moans in the mansion. When the last residents were driven out in 1900, a group bought the Octagon. The house was restored and opened to visitors. Since the remodeling, there have been fewer reports of ghosts and noises.

[29]*Haunted houses are often large. The ghosts have lots of hiding places.*

[30]One of the largest is the Winchester House in San Jose, California. For 36 years, Sarah Winchester ordered continuous building on her massive home. By the time she died in 1922, the Winchester House was a jumble of 160 rooms.

[31]Sarah was prompted by guilt. The Winchester wealth came from the sale of firearms. Sarah felt threatened by the spirits of the people who had been killed by Winchester rifles. She hoped to keep the ghostly spirits confused by the maze of construction. Stairways led nowhere. Doors opened onto blank walls or drop-offs. An elevator went up just one floor. One stairway had 7 turns and 44 steps, but rose only 9 feet. Each night Sarah rotated to a different bedroom so the ghosts could not find her.

[32]Sarah was not alone in her belief that ghosts roamed the meandering hallways of Winchester House. Workmen sighted people who would suddenly disappear.

[33]*Haunted houses have ghosts that have been witnessed by more than one person.*

[34]Even the White House is said to be haunted. Several residents and overnight guests insist they encountered Abraham Lincoln's ghost in the White House. Haunted houses don't earn much of a reputation unless the presence of a ghost is reported by lots of witnesses.

The White House

[35]What is a ghost, anyway? Believers often think ghosts represent the spirits of the dead who cannot rest. The ghosts are

earthbound for various reasons. They may be searching for something or trying to fulfill a promise. Murdered victims may wish to avenge their deaths. Or the spirits might simply want the living to be aware of their history.

[36]Parapsychologists are people who deal with events that can't be explained by present knowledge. Modern ghost hunters try to locate ghosts by using equipment such as cameras and electronic sensing devices.

[37]Skeptics respond that no gadgets can pick up evidence of ghosts. Scoffers of haunted houses claim that Jason and Kate's experience is typical. People's eyes and minds play tricks on them. This is especially true when they are already uneasy or caught off guard.

[38]Nonbelievers offer explanations for "hauntings." Lighting conditions affect what people see. In a semi-awake condition, dreamlike visions occur. Big, drafty structures produce cold spots. Wind imitates moans. Sound travels farther in cooler night air, so music might be carried from a nearby house or car. Abandoned houses shelter wildlife that could thump or make strange sounds resembling voices. Houses emit "settling" noises. They squeak, rattle, and groan.

[39]Why then, are there widespread tales of ghostly hauntings? Human beings seem to enjoy being frightened, occasionally. Scary stories have been part of different cultures for thousands of years. Maybe ghosts are connected with a belief in an afterlife. Or perhaps they simply represent the excitement involved with things we don't understand. Arguments will continue for and against the existence of ghosts.

[40]Oh, yes, another trait is shared by haunted houses.

[41]*Many haunted houses are vacant.*

[42]The reason for a vacancy is simple. No one wants to live there. Would you? Perhaps you feel like other people who have declared, "I DON'T BELIEVE IN GHOSTS—but they sure do scare me!"

If you have been timing your reading speed for this story, record your time below.

_____ : _____

Minutes   Seconds

Can You Believe This?

UNDERSTANDING THE MAIN IDEA

The following questions will demonstrate your understanding of what the story is about, or the *main idea*. Choose the best answer for each question.

1. This story is mainly about

Ⓐ a new newspaper office.

Ⓑ a horrible murder.

Ⓒ different haunted houses.

Ⓓ the haunting patterns of one ghost.

2. This story could have been titled

Ⓐ "The Debate over Haunted Houses."

Ⓑ "Laughing All the Way."

Ⓒ "One Ghost's Story."

Ⓓ "The Manchester Murders."

3. Which detail best supports the main idea of the story?

Ⓐ The father of the family got out of bed.

Ⓑ A local newspaper owner recently bought the house.

Ⓒ Many houses have a reputation of being haunted.

Ⓓ The Winchester House was a jumble of 160 rooms.

4. Find another detail that supports the main idea of this story. Write it on the lines below.

_____

_____

RECALLING FACTS

The following questions will test how well you remember the facts in the story you just read. Choose the best answer for each question.

1. Jason and Kate stayed in the deserted house because

Ⓐ their car broke down nearby.

Ⓑ they wanted to earn a reward.

Ⓒ they had just purchased the home.

Ⓓ they wanted to see a ghost.

2. Houses that are said to be haunted are

Ⓐ usually brand-new.

Ⓑ known to have a colorful past.

Ⓒ torn down right away.

Ⓓ often built by pranksters.

3. Sarah Winchester ordered continuous building on her house

Ⓐ for three years.

Ⓑ because it was too small.

Ⓒ to please her husband.

Ⓓ for 36 years.

4. Ghosts in haunted houses are usually

Ⓐ lost.

Ⓑ seen by more than one person.

Ⓒ trying to contact police.

Ⓓ imaginary.

READING BETWEEN THE LINES

An *inference* is a conclusion drawn from facts. A *generalization* is a general statement, idea, or rule that is supported by facts. Analyze the story by choosing the best answer to each question below.

1. **What conclusion can you draw from paragraph 11?**

   Ⓐ Jason and Kate wanted to burn down the house.

   Ⓑ Jason and Kate fell asleep watching TV.

   Ⓒ Jason and Kate weren't worried.

   Ⓓ Jason and Kate usually slept in sleeping bags.

2. **What conclusion can you draw from paragraph 26?**

   Ⓐ The skeleton of the woman was falling apart and the bones were hitting the wall.

   Ⓑ The owner of the house had killed the woman.

   Ⓒ The owner thought that the woman's spirit may have been haunting the house.

   Ⓓ The owner didn't want anyone to know a woman's skeleton was in the wall of his house.

3. **What generalization can you make from the story? Answer on the lines below, using complete sentences.**

   _____

   _____

   _____

   _____

   _____

   _____

4. **It can be inferred from the story that**

   Ⓐ most people enjoy ghost stories.

   Ⓑ ghosts will soon disappear completely.

   Ⓒ there are more ghosts than living humans in the world today.

   Ⓓ no one really believes in ghosts.

Can You Believe This?

DETERMINING
CAUSE AND EFFECT

Choose the best answers for the following questions to show the relationship between what happened in the story (*effects*) and why those things happened (*causes*).

1. **Because they heard strange noises every night, the family that resided in the house**

    Ⓐ hired a crew to get rid of the ghosts.

    Ⓑ started playing loud music when they went to bed.

    Ⓒ moved out of the house.

    Ⓓ tried to solve the mysterious clues left behind.

2. **What happened because Jason and Kate did not believe in ghosts?**

    Ⓐ They thought the old house should be restored.

    Ⓑ They accepted a challenge to spend the night in a haunted house.

    Ⓒ They stayed in a haunted house for ten hours even though they heard noises.

    Ⓓ They wrote a book about what causes people to imagine ghosts.

3. **Why did Sarah Winchester feel guilty?**

    Ⓐ Her family's wealth came from the sale of guns.

    Ⓑ She had killed a lot of people.

    Ⓒ She wouldn't give her money to the poor.

    Ⓓ She had taken 36 years to build a house.

4. **Why are most haunted houses empty?**

    Ⓐ Haunted houses cost so much that no one can afford to buy them.

    Ⓑ It's against the law to live in a haunted house.

    Ⓒ Everyone who lives in a haunted house gets sick.

    Ⓓ No one wants to live in a haunted house.

———■———

USING CONTEXT CLUES

Skilled readers often find the meaning of unfamiliar words by using *context clues*. This means they study the way the words are used in the text. Use the context clues in the excerpts below to determine the meaning of each **bold-faced** word. Then choose the answer that best matches the meaning of the word.

1. "By the time she [Sarah Winchester] died in 1922, the Winchester House was a **jumble** of 160 rooms."

CLUE: "[She] hoped to keep the ghostly spirits confused by the maze of construction."

  Ⓐ miniature

  Ⓑ forest

  Ⓒ mix-up

  Ⓓ replica

2. "The Winchester wealth came from the sale of **firearms**."

CLUE: "Sarah felt threatened by the spirits of the people who had been killed by Winchester rifles."

  Ⓐ flames

  Ⓑ guns

  Ⓒ alcohol

  Ⓓ clothing

3. "Sarah was not alone in her belief that ghosts roamed the **meandering** hallways of Winchester House."

CLUE: "One stairway had 7 turns and 44 steps, but rose only 9 feet."

  Ⓐ white

  Ⓑ narrow

  Ⓒ short

  Ⓓ wandering

4. "Many haunted houses are **vacant**."

CLUE: "No one wants to live there."

  Ⓐ empty

  Ⓑ expensive

  Ⓒ sad

  Ⓓ glazed

Can You Believe This?

End-of-Unit Activities

1. **All the titles in this unit ask a question relating to that article. Answer each of the titles, summarizing what you learned by reading the articles. Then write your own question that encompasses the entire unit.**

Will Cryonics Work?

_____

_____

_____

Are Crop Circles a Hoax?

_____

_____

_____

What Are Wormholes in Space?

_____

_____

_____

Who Believes in Haunted Houses?

_____

_____

_____

Unit Question:

_____

_____

_____

_____

End-of-Unit Activities

2. **Rank each of the stories in this unit, from the one you liked the most to the one you liked the least. For each story, write one interesting fact you learned. Then write a paragraph describing why you liked the story you ranked *1* the best.**

LESSON 1 Ranking _____

_____

_____

_____

LESSON 2 Ranking _____

_____

_____

_____

LESSON 3 Ranking _____

_____

_____

_____

LESSON 4 Ranking _____

_____

_____

_____

Why did you like the story you ranked *1* the best?

_____

_____

_____

_____

_____

Words-Per-Minute Chart

Directions:

Use the chart to find your words-per-minute reading speed. Refer to the reading time you recorded at the end of each article. Find your reading time in seconds along the left-hand side of the chart or minutes and seconds along the right-hand side of the chart. Your words-per-minute score will be listed next to the time in the column below the appropriate lesson number.

No. of Words	Lesson 1 1101	Lesson 2 1341	Lesson 3 1293	Lesson 4 1672	
80	826	1006	970	1254	1:20
100	661	805	776	1003	1:40
120	551	671	647	836	2:00
140	472	575	554	717	2:20
160	413	503	485	627	2:40
180	367	447	431	557	3:00
200	330	402	388	502	3:20
220	300	366	353	456	3:40
240	275	335	323	418	4:00
260	254	309	298	386	4:20
280	236	287	277	358	4:40
300	220	268	259	334	5:00
320	206	251	242	314	5:20
340	194	237	228	295	5:40
360	184	224	216	279	6:00
380	174	212	204	264	6:20
400	165	201	194	251	6:40
420	157	192	185	239	7:00
440	150	183	176	228	7:20
460	144	175	169	218	7:40
480	138	168	162	209	8:00
500	132	161	155	201	8:20
520	127	155	149	193	8:40
540	122	149	144	186	9:00
560	118	144	139	179	9:20
580	114	139	134	173	9:40
600	110	134	129	167	10:00
620	107	130	125	162	10:20
640	103	126	121	157	10:40
660	100	122	118	152	11:00
680	97	118	114	148	11:20
700	94	115	111	143	11:40
720	92	112	108	139	12:00
740	89	109	105	136	12:20
760	87	106	102	132	12:40
780	85	103	99	129	13:00
800	83	101	97	125	13:20
820	81	98	95	122	13:40
840	79	96	92	119	14:00

Seconds

Minutes and Seconds

UNIT TWO—

secrets
of the past

LESSON 5

Want to Find Lost Treasures?

Acommon human trait is the dream of finding a lost treasure. We fantasize about what our riches could buy. A big mansion. Maybe a couple of fancy cars. And some shimmering diamonds and gold jewelry, of course. The possibilities excite us. For a long time, two lost treasures have eluded recovery by aspiring millionaires.

A Treasure in Virginia

[2]What if you were given three sets of ciphers (secret writings) that guide you to a buried treasure of gold, silver, and jewels? To get you started, one of the ciphers has already been broken and the coded message translated.

[3]Sound easy? Others have thought so too. For more than 100 years people have tried to solve the two remaining ciphers. No one has claimed success.

[4]The strange treasure tale began in Virginia. In 1817 Thomas Jefferson Beale headed west as the leader of a group of 30 men. They planned to hunt buffalo. The group traveled to Santa Fe, New Mexico, a colony of the Spanish Territory at that time.

[5]The hunting party chased a herd of buffalo for a week, winding up 200 miles north of Santa Fe, near a Colorado mountain range. By chance, one of the men spotted a vein of gold. The thrilled group discovered that the area teemed with the precious metal.

[6]The men forgot the buffalo. Overcome by a violent attack of gold fever, the hunters instantly turned into gold miners. Beale and his men worked long days to recover not only gold, but silver found nearby.

[7]More than a year later it was decided to haul the riches back to Virginia. Horse-drawn wagons sagged with nearly 5,000 pounds of gold and silver.

Can You Believe This?

[8]After reaching Virginia, the group secretly buried the treasure in the foothills of the Blue Ridge Mountains. Soon Beale led the men west again to retrieve more gold and silver. Two years passed before they returned to Virginia. They added the new treasure to their earlier underground deposit.

[9]One more western journey was planned. Before leaving for a third trip, Beale handed an iron box to a trusted friend named Robert Morriss. "Open the box if I do not return within ten years," Beale said.

[10]Beale and his followers were never heard from again. Maybe thieves killed them. No one knows.

[11]Morriss didn't open the iron box for over 20 years. Finally, in 1845, he broke the lock. Inside the box were two letters from Beale, plus pages covered with numbers.

[12]Beale's letters described how he and his men found and hid the riches. Beale instructed Morriss to uncover the treasure and divide it into 31 shares. Morriss was to keep one share and split the rest with the families of the men who had buried the treasure.

[13]The pages covered with numbers were three separate coded messages. Beale's letter explained that one cipher told where to find the treasure. Another described the treasure. The last coded message listed the men whose families were entitled to a share of the wealth.

[14]Beale ended his letter by promising that a written key for breaking the codes would be mailed to Morriss. Morriss never received the key.

[15]Without the key, Morriss was unable to understand the jumble of numbers. Before he died in 1863, Morriss handed over the ciphers to his friend, James Ward.

[16]Obsessed by the challenge, Ward spent the next 20 years trying to solve the ciphers. At last he decoded cipher number two that described the treasure. It said:

[17]*I have deposited in the county of Bedford about four miles from Bufords in an excavation or vault six feet below the surface of the ground the following articles belonging jointly to the parties whose names are given in (cipher) number three herewith.*

[18]*The first deposit consisted of ten hundred and fourteen pounds of gold and thirty-eight hundred and twelve pounds of silver deposited Nov. eighteen nineteen. The second deposit was made Dec. eighteen twenty-one and consisted of nineteen*

hundred and seven pounds of gold and twelve hundred and eighty-eight of silver. Also jewels obtained in St. Louis in exchange for gold to save transportation and valued at thirteen thousand dollars.

[19]*The above is securely packed in iron pots with iron covers. The vault is roughly lined with stone, and the vessels rest on solid stone and are covered with others.*

[20]*[Cipher] number one describes the exact locality of the vault so that no difficulty will be had in finding it.*

[21]Ward solved this second cipher by realizing that it was based on the words in the Declaration of Independence. He numbered each of the 1,332 words of the Declaration. For example, the Declaration begins: "When in the course of human events . . ." Ward numbered these words 1 through 7. When a number 4 appeared in the cipher, it represented c because the 4th word in the Declaration begins with c, and so on.

[22]Ward had broken the code for the treasure's description. But he could not decipher the other two messages. The biggie, the location of the buried riches, remained a secret.

[23]In the late 1800s Thomas Jefferson Beale's ciphers were published for the general public. No one could unravel the two unsolved messages.

[24]In recent years, computers have tackled the numbers, with no luck. And the rows of numbers stump code-breaking experts.

[25]Perhaps the treasure was uncovered years ago by survivors of Beale's original group. Skeptics say the whole thing is a sham—all faked. They accuse James Ward of forging the letters and ciphers.

[26]Those who think the tale is true claim that the correct key simply has not been discovered. Believers envision heaps of gold, silver, and jewels waiting for the lucky or super-smart person who cracks the codes.

[27]Are you ready to try?

A Treasure in Arizona

[28]Another pile of gold waits for discovery. Finding the treasure known as the Lost Dutchman Mine requires not only brainpower, but also lots of legwork.

[29]You must begin your search in Arizona's menacing Superstition Mountains, east of Phoenix. Don't start packing your shovels and picks yet. First, you should know what happened to others who hunted for this well-known treasure. The history is bloody.

[30]Several versions of the Lost Dutchman Mine's past are told. So some facts are fuzzy, while others are supported.

[31]In the 1700s the wealthy Peralta family mined gold in the Superstition Mountains. The Peraltas lived in nearby Mexico. They crossed into the Spanish-owned Arizona territory for many years before being driven out by Native American Apaches.

[32]In 1866 the Peraltas abandoned the gold mine after a final battle with the Apaches. One legend says that only two Peralta men survived the fighting.

[33]Five years later, two German immigrants entered the story. The two friends, Jake Weiser and Jacob Waltz, happened to be in a Mexican village watching a card game. Suddenly the enraged losing player flashed a knife and stabbed the other man. The Germans subdued the attacker, saving the unarmed man's life.

[34]The grateful victim, only slightly wounded, was a Peralta. He rewarded his lifesavers by telling them the location of the gold mine that his family no longer operated.

[35]Weiser and Waltz found the mine in the Superstition Mountains. They were thrilled. The mine contained much more gold than the delighted partners had imagined.

[36]At this point, the tale of the Lost Dutchman Mine splits. One version says that Jake Weiser was ambushed by Apaches while Waltz was gathering supplies from the nearby small town. The other story claims that greedy Jacob Waltz murdered his partner. Whichever account is true, Weiser was killed and Waltz became the sole prospector of the gold mine.

[37]Sometimes Waltz appeared in town to swap gold for food and equipment. He became known as the "Dutchman." Townspeople whispered the news of Waltz's gold strike. Waltz knew he was followed when he returned to his mine. The scalding Arizona desert led to unfriendly mountains with twisting trails, rock slides, steep cliffs, and mean-tempered rattlesnakes. Waltz easily lost the trackers in the rugged terrain.

[38]Eventually, Jacob Waltz moved into town. He lived quietly and modestly. His neighbors doubted that he had found much gold. But before Waltz died in 1891, he boasted that the mine still glittered with plenty of gold.

[39]After Waltz's death, his friends revealed that he had dropped hints as to the location of the mine in the Superstition Mountains. Rumors

spread, and interest in the gold was renewed. Gossipers now called it the Lost Dutchman Mine.

[40]Here are some of the clues Waltz shared:

[41]*The mine is about a mile from the rock formation called Weaver's Needle.*

[42]*Locate a deep canyon running north and south. At the head of the canyon stands the ruins of an old stone building.*

[43]*A row of three mountain peaks can be seen near the mine.*

[44]*Look for a rock with a funnel-shaped opening. The hillside below the rock leads to the mine.*

[45]*The mouth of the mine faces west.*

[46]*You can see the mine only when you are almost on top of it. The mine has a chimneylike vertical shaft.*

[47]Over the years, thousands of people with gold dust in their eyes have flocked to the mountains east of Phoenix. The clues do describe some landscape features. But searchers say that putting them all together invites confusion. The landmarks are scattered helter-skelter with no apparent connections.

[48]Beware of the Superstition Mountains if you join the caravan of gold seekers. Looking for the Lost Dutchman Mine can be hazardous. Grisly murders have occurred with at least nine people killed. Two others have disappeared without a trace.

Superstition Mountains

Many people wander the dangerous trails, hopelessly lost. Accidents are common.

[49]Maybe Jacob Waltz left clues behind for a purpose. He sprinkled just enough hints to keep zealous fortune hunters scampering through the rugged mountains. Back and forth they go, like mice running a maze.

[50]What better way could Waltz keep his "Dutchman" mine lost?

If you have been timing your reading speed for this story, record your time below.

_____ : _____

Minutes   **Seconds**

UNDERSTANDING THE MAIN IDEA

The following questions will demonstrate your understanding of what the story is about, or the *main idea*. Choose the best answer for each question.

1. This story is mainly about

Ⓐ a pirate's treasure sunk in the Atlantic.

Ⓑ the best ways to find treasure.

Ⓒ two miners' treasures that were never found.

Ⓓ how to solve riddles.

2. This story could have been titled

Ⓐ "The Importance of Good Record Keeping."

Ⓑ "A Tale of Two Treasures."

Ⓒ "Treasure Lost, Then Found."

Ⓓ "Mining for Gold."

3. Which detail best supports the main idea of the story?

Ⓐ Sante Fe was a Spanish colony at that time.

Ⓑ The men secretly buried their treasure in the foothills of the Blue Mountains.

Ⓒ Jake Weiser and Jacob Waltz were watching a card game.

Ⓓ At the head of the canyon stands the ruins of an old stone building.

4. Find another detail that supports the main idea of this story. Write it on the lines below.

_____

_____

RECALLING FACTS

The following questions will test how well you remember the facts in the story you just read. Choose the best answer for each question.

1. Thomas Beale's group had planned to hunt

Ⓐ gold.

Ⓑ silver.

Ⓒ deer.

Ⓓ buffalo.

2. Thomas Beale and his men never returned from their

Ⓐ first trip.

Ⓑ second trip.

Ⓒ third trip.

Ⓓ fourth trip.

3. Thomas Beale described the location of the treasure in

Ⓐ a telephone call.

Ⓑ a riddle.

Ⓒ his diary.

Ⓓ carvings on a tree.

4. On another sheet of paper, draw a picture of the Lost Dutchman's Mine's location, using the description in the story.

———— ▬ ————

Can You Believe This?

READING BETWEEN THE LINES

An *inference* is a conclusion drawn from facts. A *generalization* is a general statement, idea, or rule that is supported by facts. Analyze the story by choosing the best answer to each question below.

1. What conclusion can you draw from paragraphs 4–6?

- Ⓐ Buffalo was more valuable than gold.
- Ⓑ The men became very ill from the gold.
- Ⓒ There was no buffalo in New Mexico.
- Ⓓ Gold was more valuable than buffalo.

2. What conclusion can you draw from paragraph 9?

- Ⓐ Beale thought he might get killed or injured.
- Ⓑ Beale wanted his friend to have all of the gold.
- Ⓒ Beale had really only found iron, not silver and gold.
- Ⓓ Beale didn't have very many friends.

3. What generalization can you make from the story?

- Ⓐ Many people will try to discover lost treasure.
- Ⓑ No one believed Beale found any gold or silver.
- Ⓒ Everyone wants to be rich.
- Ⓓ People never believe in lost treasures.

4. It can be inferred from the story that

- Ⓐ Beale didn't bury his treasure where he'd said he did.
- Ⓑ Beale didn't want the gold.
- Ⓒ the ciphers are very difficult to decode.
- Ⓓ all of the ciphers are based on historic documents.

DETERMINING CAUSE AND EFFECT

Choose the best answers for the following questions to show the relationship between what happened in the story (*effects*) and why those things happened (*causes*).

1. Because one of the men saw a vein of gold,

  Ⓐ he soon saw some silver too.

  Ⓑ the men stopped hunting buffalo.

  Ⓒ the men sent him back to Virginia.

  Ⓓ Beale and his group became lost.

2. What happened because Robert Morriss didn't have the key to the ciphers?

  Ⓐ The treasure was found almost immediately.

  Ⓑ Morriss burned the letters and the ciphers.

  Ⓒ Morriss got the ciphers from Beale.

  Ⓓ Morriss couldn't understand the ciphers.

3. Why did the Peralta men abandon the gold mine?

  Ⓐ The mine wasn't in Mexico.

  Ⓑ It was too hard to get across the border.

  Ⓒ All the gold had already been mined.

  Ⓓ There were battles with some fierce Apaches.

4. Why did Jacob Waltz's neighbors think he hadn't found much gold?

  Ⓐ He lived modestly.

  Ⓑ He said he hadn't found much.

  Ⓒ His partner stole all the gold.

  Ⓓ No one could find the mine.

———■———

USING CONTEXT CLUES

Skilled readers often find the meaning of unfamiliar words by using *context clues*. This means they study the way the words are used in the text. Use the context clues in the excerpts below to determine the meaning of each **bold-faced** word. Then choose the answer that best matches the meaning of the word.

1. "For a long time, two lost treasures have **eluded** recovery by aspiring millionaires."

CLUE: "No one has claimed success."

Ⓐ lost

Ⓑ escaped

Ⓒ had

Ⓓ confused

2. "Beale's letter explained that one **cipher** told where to find the treasure."

CLUE: "The pages covered with numbers were three separate coded messages."

Ⓐ beverage

Ⓑ problem

Ⓒ solution

Ⓓ riddle

3. "The Germans **subdued** the attacker, saving the unarmed man's life."

CLUE: "The grateful victim, only slightly wounded, was a Peralta."

Ⓐ overcame

Ⓑ quiet

Ⓒ helped

Ⓓ left

4. "Waltz easily lost the trackers in the rugged **terrain**."

CLUE: "The scalding Arizona desert led to unfriendly mountains with twisting trails, rock slides, steep cliffs, and mean-tempered rattlesnakes."

Ⓐ landscape

Ⓑ vehicle

Ⓒ house

Ⓓ city

LESSON 6

Do Cannibals and Headhunters Exist?

You've probably seen the cartoons. Jungle savages dance around a huge pot of water that hangs over a fire. Sitting in the big cooking pot is a fully dressed man. He dared to trespass into the territory of the cannibals. The man, more surprised than scared, is the main ingredient for the "soup of the day."

[2]This represents a typical cannibal cartoon, but do people actually eat the flesh of other humans?

[3]Yes, there are crazed individuals who have murdered and consumed their victims. Thankfully, these insane killers are rare.

[4]Cannibalism horrifies us. In some cases, however, survivors of disasters had no choice but to eat their dead companions. Otherwise, the survivors would have starved to death. Conditions of severe hunger have convinced society to forgive the grisly deeds.

[5]But has cannibalism ever been an accepted custom by groups of people? Ancient Chinese said the Koreans were cannibals. Koreans accused the Chinese of the same thing. The 16th-century Spanish conquistadors described how the Aztecs of Central America butchered, cooked, and devoured their enemies. Aztecs claimed the invaders from Spain were actually the wicked cannibals.

[6]One group accuses another group of being barbarians and cannibals. Is this just the way people hurl the ultimate insult at other cultures? Or are there truths in some reports?

[7]In recent centuries we find scattered accounts of cannibals and headhunters. Here are some of them.

Papua New Guinea

[8]Papua New Guinea is part of an island that lies in the southern Pacific Ocean. It is north of Australia and just south of the equator. Much of the land is rugged with thick jungles, crocodile-infested rivers, swamps, and mountains with high plateaus. Steep cliffs border narrow, winding valleys.

[9]In these harsh surroundings, a few tribes of people stayed totally isolated from the outside world until the 1930s. Up to that time, some primitive people lived as their ancestors had thousands of years ago.

[10]A big part of the culture was warfare. Bloody wars resulted from conflicts over land. Even a small squabble, like a stolen pig, could heat up into a fierce battle where hundreds of warriors clashed.

[11]Ongoing warfare led to headhunting. When one fighter killed another, the victim's head was chopped off and collected as a trophy. The most respected warrior owned the most heads.

[12]A tribe in the western highlands, the Biamis, displayed skulls of their victims. The skulls decorated village huts. Another tribe called the Asmat showed off their trophies by mounting the heads on poles.

[13]The people of the Sepik River shot enemies with poisoned arrows. Once they had a reputation as brutal headhunters who ate their victims, but today they are peaceful.

[14]Both cannibalism and headhunting were outlawed in Papua New Guinea several years ago. The last cases were reported in the early 1960s.

A New Guinea Cannibal Chief

[15]Among a few clans, a type of cannibalism continues today. It is a religious rite at a funeral. When a father or mother dies, the children might eat a tiny bit of flesh as a ritual. They believe that the spirit is recycled. The powers of one

generation are then passed to the next.

[16]Two groups, the Hewa and the Fore, have a similar belief. Small amounts of a dead person's body are eaten by relatives to release the spirit from the body.

[17]In areas where these rites continue, a disease called kuru is blamed on the cannibalism. Kuru is a fatal "laughing disease" that affects the nervous system. It is said to be transmitted one way—by eating body parts of an infected person. The virus causes stages of uncontrollable laughing, screaming, and shaking. An agonizing death usually results.

Fiji

[18]Fiji consists of more than 300 small islands sprinkled in the South Pacific, 2,000 miles east of Australia. The islands are an ideal tropical paradise. By the 19th century, though, the outside world called some of the islands the "Cannibal Isles."

[19]The bad reputation started in 1789. An Englishman, Fletcher Christian, led a famous mutiny aboard the big sailing ship HMS *Bounty*. William Bligh, the ship's captain, was cast adrift in a small boat with 18 faithful sailors. The men landed on Fiji's Yasawa Island. Their delight with the beautiful surroundings quickly changed to terror. Local natives turned out to be unfriendly cannibals. Captain Bligh and his men bolted back to their boat and paddled away. One sailor was left behind. Legend says the natives captured him because he was the fattest Englishman and would make a tasty meal.

[20]Years later, anthropologists— scientists who study human beings— interviewed natives of Fiji. Many Fijians thought the stories of cannibalism were propaganda. Boasting ancestors exaggerated their dirty deeds to prevent invasion of their islands.

Borneo

[21]Borneo is an Indonesian island south of the Philippines. Various tribes carried out headhunting for different reasons. Some warriors thought that headhunting gave them strength and proved their bravery.

[22]For other tribes, headhunting had religious meanings. Warriors displayed skulls in their huts believing they would bring strength and prosperity to the family. Members of the family fed the spirit that dwelled within a skull by stuffing the mouth, eyes, and nose with bits of food.

[23]In 1959, Indonesian lawmakers outlawed headhunting.

Ecuador

[24]The country of Ecuador is located in the northwest part of South America. The Shuar people of the Amazon rain forest were known headhunters for hundreds, perhaps thousands, of years. They hacked off an enemy's head and then went a step further. They would then shrink the head.

[25]In Shuar society, violence was the leading cause of death. One-third of all deaths were from battle wounds.

[26]In the 15th century, the mighty Inca empire tried to claim the Shuar's territory. But they were defeated by the defiant Shuar tribes. In the 16th century, the invading Spaniards were also driven out by the fearless Shuar.

[27]Not until the 20th century were outsiders able to have peaceful contact with the Shuar. Anthropologists learned details about the gruesome methods of shrinking heads.

[28]During the frequent warfare, the Shuar warriors collected opponents' heads. They thought shrinking the heads would keep the outraged spirits of the dead from coming back.

[29]First, a warrior removed the skull. He packed hot sand in the skulless head. This made it start shrinking. Then he grasped the hair and dipped the head in hot water. This caused the skin to shrink more. Drying came next. Last, the eyes and mouth were sewn shut. This was to trap the victim's vengeful spirit inside the shrunken head. The finished trophy-head shriveled to about half its original size.

[30]The practice of head shrinking had already ended in Ecuador when laws against headhunting were passed in the 1970s.

[31]Scattered civilizations seem to have taken part in the dreadful customs of cannibalism and headhunting. Is this really true? The act of headhunting is not challenged. Shrunken heads, now mostly found in museums, are reminders of this gory sport. But what about cannibalism?

[32]Researchers have been rethinking this one. Throughout the ages, people lashed out at others by accusing them of being cruel cannibals. It's agreed that there have been occasions of cannibalism. The argument is over the question: Has cannibalism been a common custom for a group of people?

[33]No—it's a myth, according to some scientists. They claim the folklore grew from the desire of one culture to feel superior to another.

These same critics point out that no reliable witnesses ever directly observed a cannibal feast. Oddly, the information was always at least second- or third-hand. And researchers usually reported that the practice stopped at a time in the past.

[34]Gullible anthropologists are blamed for spreading rumors invented by tribes against their hated rivals. Skeptics declare it's unfair to tag a group as cannibals when there is no proof.

[35]The uproar continues. Some anthropologists defend the opinion that cannibalism goes back as far as prehistoric times. The most recent evidence comes from a cave in France.

[36]Neanderthal bones about 100,000 years old were found. The bones were from six individuals and bore deliberate cuts. Tim White of the University of California, Berkeley, examined the bones.

According to White, "The markings were what you'd expect if you were slicing up and down to cut the meat away from a turkey bone." Skulls were smashed to remove the brains, and bones were broken for the marrow. Even so, it is not known if this was a common practice or a single event.

[37]Other recent evidence challenges whether modern humans are even directly descended from Neanderthals. The simmering debates will go on as new scientific information is discovered.

[38]A glance at the dark side of human behavior jolts us. We're shocked by cannibalism and headhunting. At the same time, we're fascinated. Perhaps we take comfort in thinking that such primitive behavior is outside our own culture's door. Labeling the acts as intolerable by society helps define our views of civilized humanity.

If you have been timing your reading speed for this story, record your time below.

_____ : _____

Minutes   **Seconds**

UNDERSTANDING THE MAIN IDEA

The following questions will demonstrate your understanding of what the story is about, or the *main idea*. Choose the best answer for each question.

1. This story is mainly about

Ⓐ the cannibals in the world today.

Ⓑ the history of tales about cannibals and headhunting.

Ⓒ the practice of shrinking heads in South America.

Ⓓ the medicinal properties of headhunting and cannibalism.

2. This story could have been titled

Ⓐ "The Roots of Cannibalistic and Headhunting Stories."

Ⓑ "The Earliest Cannibals."

Ⓒ "Neanderthal Religious Rites."

Ⓓ "Beware of the Headhunters."

3. Which detail best supports the main idea of the story?

Ⓐ Much of Papua New Guinea is covered with jungles, rivers, swamps, and mountains.

Ⓑ Cannibalism and headhunting were outlawed years ago.

Ⓒ Fijians think their ancestors made up their cannibalistic practices.

Ⓓ One-third of all Shuar deaths were due to wounds from battles.

4. Find another detail that supports the main idea of this story. Write it on the lines below.

_____

_____

RECALLING FACTS

The following questions will test how well you remember the facts in the story you just read. Choose the best answer for each question.

1. Tribes on Papua New Guinea cut off their victims' heads to

Ⓐ prevent the victim from coming back to life.

Ⓑ make sure the victim was welcomed by the gods.

Ⓒ decorate their canoes.

Ⓓ display as trophies.

2. A few clans practice a type of cannibalism as

Ⓐ a way to prevent hunger.

Ⓑ a way to scare their ancestors.

Ⓒ a religious practice.

Ⓓ publicity stunts.

3. The Shuar would

Ⓐ shrink their victims' heads.

Ⓑ avoid war at all costs.

Ⓒ sacrifice themselves to a headhunting tribe.

Ⓓ sell shrunken heads to tourists.

4. No one has ever observed a

Ⓐ shrunken head.

Ⓑ cannibalistic feast.

Ⓒ war between tribes.

Ⓓ victim being buried.

Can You Believe This?

READING BETWEEN THE LINES

An *inference* is a conclusion drawn from facts. A *generalization* is a general statement, idea, or rule that is supported by facts. Analyze the story by choosing the best answer to each question below.

1. What conclusion can you draw from paragraph 10?

   Ⓐ Papua New Guinea was a peaceful place.

   Ⓑ Residents were trying to modernize their cities.

   Ⓒ The police in Papua New Guinea weren't effective.

   Ⓓ Tribes fought each other often.

2. What conclusion can you draw from paragraphs 18–19?

   Ⓐ Fijians wanted to develop tourism.

   Ⓑ Fijians worshiped the man left behind by Bligh.

   Ⓒ Bligh and his men wanted to live on Fiji.

   Ⓓ Fijians were worried about European invaders.

3. What generalization can you make from the story?

   Ⓐ Few tribes practice any type of cannibalism today.

   Ⓑ Everyone knows the Shuar are cannibals.

   Ⓒ All Spanish conquistadors practiced cannibalism.

   Ⓓ It's common to see shrunken heads in Papua New Guinea.

4. Write an inference about cannibalism and headhunting that can be made from this story.

_____

_____

_____

_____

_____

_____

—— ▬ ——

DETERMINING
CAUSE AND EFFECT

Choose the best answers for the following questions to show the relationship between what happened in the story (*effects*) and why those things happened (*causes*).

1. **Because a few Papua New Guinea tribes stayed isolated until the 1930s, they**

   Ⓐ lived just as their ancestors had.

   Ⓑ were unaware that headhunting was a common practice.

   Ⓒ fought a lot with other tribes.

   Ⓓ don't travel much even today.

2. **What happened because some sailors reported that Fijians were cannibals?**

   Ⓐ A lot of people traveled to Fiji.

   Ⓑ Fiji became known as the "Cannibal Isles."

   Ⓒ An international group went to Fiji to educate the residents.

   Ⓓ No one ever went to Fiji again.

3. **Why did warriors in Borneo display skulls in their huts?**

   Ⓐ Skulls were considered to be very beautiful.

   Ⓑ They wanted to scare their children.

   Ⓒ They believed it would lead to strength and prosperity.

   Ⓓ Indonesian lawmakers outlawed headhunting.

4. **Why is headhunting known to have happened?**

   Ⓐ People talk about it a lot.

   Ⓑ The Shuar were very violent.

   Ⓒ It often goes hand-in-hand with cannibalism.

   Ⓓ There is historical proof.

——— ■ ———

USING CONTEXT CLUES

Skilled readers often find the meaning of unfamiliar words by using *context clues*. This means they study the way the words are used in the text. Use the context clues in the excerpts below to determine the meaning of each **bold-faced** word. Then choose the answer that best matches the meaning of the word.

1. "It [a type of cannibalism] is a religious **rite** at a funeral."

CLUE: "When a father or mother dies, the children might eat a tiny bit of flesh as a ritual."

   Ⓐ ceremonial act

   Ⓑ freedom to act

   Ⓒ blessing

   Ⓓ feast

2. "An Englishman . . . led a famous **mutiny** aboard the big sailing ship HMS *Bounty*."

CLUE: "William Bligh, the ship's captain, was cast adrift in a small boat with 18 faithful sailors."

   Ⓐ play

   Ⓑ crew

   Ⓒ rebellion

   Ⓓ horse

3. "Many Fijians thought the stories of cannibalism were **propaganda**."

CLUE: "Boasting ancestors exaggerated their dirty deeds to prevent invasion of their islands."

   Ⓐ dreams

   Ⓑ lies

   Ⓒ true

   Ⓓ funny

4. "The bones were from six individuals and bore **deliberate** cuts."

CLUE: ". . . 'The markings were what you'd expect if you were slicing up and down to cut the meat away from a turkey bone.' "

   Ⓐ accidental

   Ⓑ complete

   Ⓒ slow

   Ⓓ purposeful

Can You Believe This?

Why Do Egyptian Mummies Fascinate Us?

Visit a museum that displays mummies, and you'll find they are one of the most popular exhibits. Mummies lure curious onlookers. Why?

[2]Mummies are simply dead bodies that have been preserved. But dead bodies arouse our curiosity in a morbid way. Even dead animals next to the highway get our attention. We don't want to stare, yet we do.

[3]With a mummy of a fellow human being, the fascination is more personal. We wonder: How did the person die? How long ago? How was the body preserved?

[4]When a person or animal dies, the natural process of decaying begins. But this process can be prevented one of three ways: freezing, drying, or with the use of chemicals.

[5]Over the years, mummies have been found that have formed naturally. Preserved bodies are discovered frozen in icy places. In high mountain areas, cold winds dry out bodies, forming natural mummies. Ancient human remains turn up in European peat bogs. The rotted plants in marshy bogs produce acids that preserve, or "pickle," the bodies.

[6]Besides these natural mummies, people have been mummified deliberately. The most famous of these are the mummies of Egypt.

[7]The ancient Egyptian civilization began about 5,000 years ago and lasted for more than 3,000 years. During their long history, Egyptians built magnificent structures like the pyramids. They also gave us statues, paintings, and writings called hieroglyphics. And they made mummies. Millions of mummies.

[8]People have accused the ancient Egyptians of being obsessed with death. It can be argued that the opposite is true. They enjoyed life so much that they wanted to live forever. Preserving dead bodies was a part of their religion. Egyptians believed that being mummified was necessary to enter the afterlife. They thought that the spirit of the dead person returned to its body to rest at night. The body had to look as it did when alive so the spirit could recognize it.

[9]In the beginning of the Egyptian civilization, the Egyptians buried the deceased in the desert sand. People were arranged on their sides with the knees bent. A few items, like clay pots, were placed nearby. Early Egyptians probably observed that bodies dried out in the scalding desert sand.

[10]Soon experiments with mummification began. At first, the embalmers just wrapped linen strips around the dead person. This did not work. It made decay worse by keeping the body damp, allowing bacteria to grow. Embalmers tried new methods, eventually finding ways to mummify that worked.

[11]Not everyone could afford the services of the embalmers. When people died, most of them continued to be buried in desert graves. For wealthy Egyptians though, three different levels of mummification were offered. The two lower levels were used for court officials and others who could pay the costs. But the highest level was reserved for royalty. This deluxe procedure took 70 days.

[12]The ancient embalmers did not leave directions for making mummies, but their secrets were shared. A Greek writer, Herodotus, visited Egypt in 484 B.C. He was allowed to view an elaborate mummification and write down what he saw. What did he tell us about mummy-making?

[13]Priests chanted magic spells and prayers throughout the embalming process. A large mask of a jackal covered the chief priest's head. He represented Anubis, the jackal-headed god of embalming.

[14]First, the body was washed. Then the chief priest of the embalmers made a cut in the left side of the body. He removed the internal organs—lungs, liver, stomach, and intestines. Embalmers covered the body parts with resin—a liquid made from plant gum that hardens when dry. They stored the body parts separately in canopic jars. These special clay jars were topped

with lids shaped to look like the heads of animals or people.

[15]The heart remained inside the chest. Ancient Egyptians believed that the heart produced thoughts and feelings. They also believed that the gods weighed the heart before the person entered the afterlife. The heart's weight determined if the individual had lived a good life on Earth.

[16]Egyptians did not understand the function or importance of the brain. It was simply removed and thrown away. To remove it, a thin rod with a hooked end was inserted through the nostrils to scoop out brain tissue.

[17]Embalmers then cleaned the body inside and out with palm wine and spices. Next came the most important step, drying out the body. It was packed in a type of powdery salt called natron. The corpse rested on a slanted table so that fluids could drain. For the next 40 days, the body lay undisturbed.

[18]At the end of 40 days, embalmers removed the body from the natron and rubbed the leathery skin with perfumed oils. They stuffed the withered torso with cloth pads, sand, or mud, to make it look more natural. Priests sealed the nose and mouth with beeswax. They packed linen in the eye sockets. Royal fingers and toes were encased with individual gold covers before the next procedure, the wrapping.

[19]Wrapping the corpse took up to 15 days. Using resin-soaked linen strips, the embalmers bandaged each finger and toe. Then they wound strips around the head, torso, arms, and legs. More liquid resin and perfumed oils stiffened the wrappings. The priests inserted good-luck charms between the linen layers to protect the dead person. Some amulets were symbols, such as a tiny set of stairs representing steps leading to the afterlife. Small statues of the gods were common. Another popular amulet was the scarab, a beetle carved out of a gemstone. The scarab represented rebirth.

[20]Embalmers wrapped a wide bandage around the entire body. They coated it with more oils and resin. The chief priest placed a mask of the person's face over the wrapped head to help the spirit recognize it.

[21]An important ceremony followed. It was called the Opening of the Mouth. This ritual allowed the soul to reenter the body. Now the dead person could eat, drink, and speak in the afterlife.

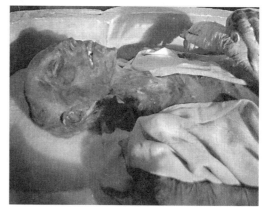

The mummified remains of Ramses II in Cairo, Egypt

[22]The mummy was finished. The priests placed the mummy in a formfitting case. It was painted with pictures and writings. Magic spells provided protection from evil. The mummy case fit inside another, slightly larger, decorated coffin.

[23]Professional mourners were paid to cry loudly as the body was moved to a tomb. The coffin finally rested inside a large stone container, a sarcophagus, inscribed with more magic spells.

[24]Unfortunately, the charms and spells did not protect the mummies. Grave robbers looted the tombs of the wealthy, especially royal tombs. The pyramids were built to hold the bodies of early pharaohs (kings), but the structures were soon invaded.

[25]New burial sites were chiseled out of rock in steep cliffs known as the Valley of the Kings. The barren site lies along the southern part of the Nile River. But as before, thieves plundered the tombs.

[26]Only one tomb of a pharaoh has ever been found that was not robbed—the grave of King Tutankhamen, or King Tut. The sealed tomb, discovered in 1922, held magnificent treasures. Stacked in one chamber were hundreds of priceless objects like statues, furniture, and jewelry. In the connecting burial chamber a huge gilded shrine surrounded King Tut's ornate sarcophagus. Three coffins nested within the stone sarcophagus. A gold innermost coffin held the mummy of the young king. The death mask covering the mummy's head was breathtaking—solid gold, inlaid with jewels and tiny pieces of colored glass.

[27]King Tut was an unimportant ruler who died more than 3,000 years ago, when he was just 18 years old. We can only imagine what fantastic riches were buried with more important pharaohs who ruled longer.

[28]Ancient Egyptians also mummified animals for religious reasons. People believed that many animals were sacred—cats, birds, monkeys, reptiles, even insects.

[29]Eventually, the practice of making mummies tapered off. Religious beliefs changed. By the

seventh century A.D., mummification ended. But what happened to the millions of mummies that had been made earlier?

[30]Although some are now kept in museums around the world, most were destroyed. In the 13th century, medieval Europeans wrongly believed that an ingredient in mummy wrappings healed illnesses. They made medicines by grinding pieces of stiff linen strips into a powder. Eventually the entire mummy, including the body, was ground up. People put mummy powder on wounds. They even ate it as a cure-all. Sometimes they mixed the powder with water, then drank it. Swallowing mummy powder often caused stomach cramps and vomiting. But for the next 400 years, some people continued the gruesome practice of consuming mummy powder.

[31]Mummies were treated in other undignified ways. Some ended up as fertilizer. Many were burned for fuel. Travelers bought mummies as souvenirs. In the 1800s, unwrapping a mummy was a popular entertainment. Afterward, the mummy was discarded.

[32]In recent years the remaining mummies have finally been treated with respect. Only on rare occasions do scientists unwrap a mummy. Then a team of experts handles the body with care. They can tell a mummy's age at death, figure its blood type, and find signs of arthritis or other diseases. Usually they can find out what caused the person's death.

[33]Today it's no longer necessary to disturb the bandages to "see" the body. CAT scanning machines, aided by computers, give a detailed model of the skeleton. With this knowledge, experts reconstruct how the person looked before death. In a sense, the mummy is brought "back to life."

[34]Like time capsules, mummies give us a peek at the past. They give us clues about an advanced civilization from thousands of years ago. Ancient Egyptians wanted to live forever. Through their pyramids, artwork, writings, and mummies— they are still alive.

If you have been timing your reading speed for this story, record your time below.

_____ : _____

Minutes   *Seconds*

UNDERSTANDING THE MAIN IDEA

The following questions will demonstrate your understanding of what the story is about, or the *main idea*. Choose the best answer for each question.

1. This story is mainly about

ⓐ medicine made from mummy powder.

ⓑ the jewels buried with mummies.

ⓒ tomb robbers.

ⓓ ancient Egyptian mummies.

2. This story could have been titled

ⓐ "Preparing Mummies."

ⓑ "Weird Uses for Mummies."

ⓒ "Bringing the Dead Back to Life."

ⓓ "Roman Mummies."

3. Which detail best supports the main idea of the story?

ⓐ Rotted plants in marshy bogs preserve bodies.

ⓑ Egyptians built pyramids.

ⓒ Embalmers dried out the bodies, an important step in mummification.

ⓓ Not everyone could afford the services of embalmers.

4. Find another detail that supports the main idea of this story. Write it on the lines below.

_____

_____

RECALLING FACTS

The following questions will test how well you remember the facts in the story you just read. Choose the best answer for each question.

1. Mummies can be preserved naturally through

ⓐ baking.

ⓑ freezing.

ⓒ burying.

ⓓ wetting.

2. Egyptians thought being mummified was necessary to

ⓐ prevent disease.

ⓑ enter the afterlife.

ⓒ please their ancestors.

ⓓ stay alive.

3. Embalmers did not remove the

ⓐ liver.

ⓑ lungs.

ⓒ heart.

ⓓ brain.

4. The most important step in mummification was

ⓐ wrapping.

ⓑ decorating.

ⓒ drying.

ⓓ burying.

READING BETWEEN THE LINES

An *inference* is a conclusion drawn from facts. A *generalization* is a general statement, idea, or rule that is supported by facts. Analyze the story by choosing the best answer to each question below.

1. What conclusion can you draw from paragraphs 13–15?

Ⓐ Mummification was a religious process.

Ⓑ There were many wealthy Egyptians.

Ⓒ It was considered unclean to touch the right side of a body.

Ⓓ Egyptians thought their organs would turn into animals.

2. What conclusion can you draw from paragraphs 24–25?

Ⓐ The Valley of the Kings is a popular tourist site.

Ⓑ The pyramids became full after a while.

Ⓒ The families of the dead person often robbed the tombs.

Ⓓ Egyptians hoped rock burial sites would stop grave robbers.

3. What generalization can you make from the story?

Ⓐ All Egyptians knew how to make mummies.

Ⓑ Many Egyptians wanted to live in the afterlife.

Ⓒ Few Egyptians were buried.

Ⓓ All mummies are Egyptian.

4. It can be inferred from the story that

Ⓐ the wealthiest Egyptians had the most elaborate burial chambers.

Ⓑ the poorest Egyptians often became mummies.

Ⓒ a lot of dead Egyptians were thrown into the Nile.

Ⓓ many Egyptian children wanted to be priests.

———■———

DETERMINING CAUSE AND EFFECT

Choose the best answers for the following questions to show the relationship between what happened in the story (*effects*) and why those things happened (*causes*).

1. Because cold winds dry out bodies,

Ⓐ mountain residents often take their loved ones to the lowlands for burial.

Ⓑ natural mummies have been found in high mountain areas.

Ⓒ ancient bodies have been found in peat bogs.

Ⓓ the Egyptians used fans to make mummies.

2. What happened because not everyone could afford to be embalmed?

Ⓐ Many children became slaves to pay for their parents' mummifications.

Ⓑ Embalmers decided to work for free.

Ⓒ Most people were buried in the desert.

Ⓓ Embalmers were the wealthiest Egyptians.

3. Why did ancient Egyptians leave the heart in the body? Answer on the lines below, using complete sentences.

_____

_____

_____

_____

_____

_____

4. Why was a mummy's mouth opened at the end of mummification?

Ⓐ The soul could then reenter the body.

Ⓑ Evil spirits needed to escape.

Ⓒ The mummy would speak to the priests.

Ⓓ Valuable jewels were hidden in the mouth.

———■———

Can You Believe This?

USING CONTEXT CLUES

Skilled readers often find the meaning of unfamiliar words by using *context clues*. This means they study the way the words are used in the text. Use the context clues in the excerpts below to determine the meaning of each **bold-faced** word. Then choose the answer that best matches the meaning of the word.

1. "But this process [of decay] can be **prevented** one of three ways: freezing, drying, or with the use of chemicals."

CLUE: "Preserved bodies are discovered frozen in icy places."

Ⓐ stopped

Ⓑ speeded

Ⓒ helped

Ⓓ caught

2. "He [a Greek writer] was allowed to view an **elaborate** mummification and write down what he saw."

CLUE: "This deluxe procedure took 70 days."

Ⓐ quick

Ⓑ expensive

Ⓒ complicated

Ⓓ simple

3. "Some **amulets** were symbols, such as a tiny set of stairs."

CLUE: "The priests inserted good-luck charms between the linen layers to protect the dead person."

Ⓐ bracelets

Ⓑ lucky pieces

Ⓒ perfumes

Ⓓ wrappings

4. "Mummies were treated in other **undignified** ways."

CLUE: "Some ended up as fertilizer. Many were burned for fuel. Travelers bought mummies as souvenirs."

Ⓐ disrespectful

Ⓑ sophisticated

Ⓒ interesting

Ⓓ neat

———■———

Can You Believe This?

Who or What Is El Dorado?

Fom Spanish, El Dorado is translated as "The Golden Man," or "The Golden King." Sometimes, El Dorado is considered a *place*—a hidden city full of golden treasures.

[2] The legend of El Dorado is over 450 years old. Like other legends, there's no proof that the stories are true. But many people believe the El Dorado legend is based on fact.

[3] This version is often told:

High in the mountains, near a beautiful lake, a group of people lived in a peaceful kingdom. Once each year, the people held a sacred ceremony. Their chief became the Golden Man. Servants smeared a sticky substance on the chief's skin. Then they sprinkled gold dust over his entire body. The gilded chief sat on a throne that was placed upon a raft. Attendants rowed him to the middle of the lake. The chief threw golden objects, jewelry, and emeralds into the water as offerings to the gods. On shore, a chorus sang and played instruments while people tossed more gold offerings into the lake. Finally, the chief dove into the water to wash off the gold dust. Afterward, everyone celebrated by feasting and dancing.

[4] Some historians think the ceremony was actually performed by a group that lived long ago. They lived in the Andes Mountains in what is now Colombia, South America.

[5] High in the Colombian mountains is Lake Guatavita, which might be the sacred site. Its mirrorlike surface reflects the sunlight. To the people, entering the water was like entering the spirit world. When the chief passed through the lake's shiny surface, he performed a religious ritual. He made contact between the real and spirit worlds.

[6]The Lake Guatavita ceremony ended around 1480. The people vanished after another group invaded the region. But stories of the lake ritual lived on, even after the arrival of the Europeans.

[7]Sailing from Spain in 1492, Christopher Columbus landed in the New World. By mistake, Columbus called the natives *Indians*. Columbus thought he'd landed near the Indies (today's India, Japan, and China). Before he left the New World, trading Indians gave Columbus gifts of gold. After Columbus returned to Spain, people spread the exciting news, "The New World is rich with gold!"

[8]In the 1500s, Spanish soldiers called *conquistadors* flooded into what is now South America. Their mission was to explore, conquer lands, and claim all of the riches they could find—especially gold.

[9]The Indians of South America were skilled at making gold jewelry and decorative objects. Sometimes they used gold in religious ceremonies. Gold was admired because it resembled the color and brilliance of the sun. But the natives did not share the Europeans' ideas about its value. Gold did not represent wealth to the Indians. Unfortunately, they would find out just how much it meant to the invaders from across the sea.

[10]*Gold fever* can be a dangerous disease. It raged out of control in South America. By the 1530s, the Inca Empire had surrendered to Spanish soldiers. Conquistadors loaded large amounts of gold on ships headed for Spain. It was not enough. Rumors swirled that even more treasures waited for discovery.

[11]Some tales described the ancient ceremony of the golden man and the lake littered with gold and emeralds. Other stories described a city so rich that the streets were paved with gold.

[12]It was February 1541. The location was Quito, in present-day Ecuador, on the western coast of South America. A conquistador named Gonzalo Pizarro prepared to depart, leading 220 Spanish soldiers. The men were heavily armed with muskets, crossbows, and swords. Some soldiers rode horses, while others walked. Hopes were high for a rewarding adventure.

[13]Pizarro and his men believed that a city of gold awaited them. They heard that El Dorado was a kingdom hidden in the unchartered rain forest, east of Quito. But their dreams of gold would soon melt into a nightmarish journey.

[14]The conquistadors forced 4,000 Indians to go with them to act as guides and to carry supplies. They loaded heavy baggage on the backs of hundreds of llamas. For food, 4,000 pigs were taken along. Nearly 1,000 trained attack dogs accompanied the soldiers to keep the Indians from escaping.

[15]After leaving the mountainous town of Quito, the long caravan wound down into the rain forest. Indians used machetes to hack a trail through thick tangles of plants and trees. Progress was slow.

[16]Day after day they trudged through the rain forest. Many Indians died. Used to living in cold mountain villages, they could not survive the harsh conditions in the tropical rain forest. Furry-coated llamas also began to die.

[17]Conditions were miserable. Daily rains battered the men and animals. Between downpours, the blazing sun turned the rain forest into a steam bath. Horses slipped on the muddy paths. Soldiers sweltered in body armor and metal helmets. Poisonous snakes infested the thick vegetation and struck when disturbed. Thousands of annoying insects swarmed and bit. Mosquitoes spread a deadly disease—malaria. Men grew weak with high fevers.

[18]From time to time, the conquistadors discovered Indian tribes living in rain forest villages. The soldiers demanded, "Where is El Dorado? Where is the gold?" Terrified natives did not know the answer but found a way to get rid of the invaders. The soldiers were told that what they sought was just a few days' march away. Villagers pointed to a direction, and the army moved on, deeper into the rain forest.

[19]Some villagers fiercely resisted the Europeans. When skirmishes broke out, soldiers fired their muskets and crossbows. The Indians shot back with poisoned arrows that caused a painful, slow death. But the Indians' weapons were no match for those of Pizarro and his men.

[20]After months of slow traveling, the conquistadors reached a big river that would later be named the Amazon. The men met scary water creatures. Crocodilelike caimans lurked in the water, waiting for a meal. When men or animals fell into the river, the reptiles grabbed the victims and dragged them underwater.

[21]The smell of blood in the water attracted piranhas, flesh-eating fish with deadly teeth. If a caiman didn't finish its meal, piranhas quickly swam in to clean up the leftovers.

Gonzalo Pizarro

The sharp teeth and aggressive behavior of the fish intimidated the soldiers.

[22]More than a year had passed since the weary travelers left Quito. After zigzagging through the rain forest, they had not found a city of gold. Food was scarce. All of the llamas had died long ago. Most of the captive Indians had either died or escaped.

[23]The men cut down trees to build a large boat. For metal parts, they used the shoes of dead horses. Pizarro gave orders to his trusted captain, Francisco de Orellana. "Take 60 men with you and float down the river to find food. Return quickly."

[24]When Orellana and his party left, the boat swept downstream. They would not be able to return. The current was too strong. The boat carried them across the South American continent. At stops along the way, the hungry soldiers met friendly Indians who showed them how to find rain forest plants they could eat.

[25]After a five-month voyage, Orellana's group reached the east coast and the Atlantic Ocean. It was September 1542, 18 months after the entire group had departed Quito, on the west side of the continent.

[26]Meanwhile, Pizarro gave up on Orellana's returning with food. Pizarro and his starving men staggered back to Quito. They had eaten the horses, dogs, even leather. Their clothes hung in tatters on bodies covered with scars and sores.

[27]After enduring 18 months of misery, the total survivors numbered less than half of the original 220 conquistadors. They sailed back to Spain empty-handed.

[28]But the harsh sufferings of Pizarro and his men did not halt future expeditions. Throughout the 1500s, Spanish explorers searched for the elusive El Dorado. Questions

continued. Was it a mysterious city filled with gold? Or was El Dorado the gilded chief who threw offerings into the lake?

[29]Many people stuck to the belief that El Dorado referred to the Lake Guatavita ceremony. In 1580, a Spaniard named Don Antonia Sepulveda tried to drain the lake. He used Indian workers to cut a trench in a wall of the lake, allowing water to escape. Sepulveda found only one emerald and several gold objects. One day, walls of dirt suddenly collapsed, killing many workers. Sepulveda abandoned the project.

[30]Over the years, others attempted to uncover the lake's secrets. Treasure hunters tried diving, drilling, and digging. A few gold objects turned up, but not enough to pay for the projects. Finally in 1965, the Colombian government banned all lake explorations by declaring the lake a historical site.

[31]Not long afterward, in 1969, a fascinating discovery turned up in a cave near Lake Guatavita. It was an 8-inch solid gold model of a raft. In the center, a tall figure of a "Golden King" sat on a throne, surrounded by tiny figures of oarsmen. The ancient object made doubters reconsider that the El Dorado legend might be true.

[32]Even today, adventurers travel to South America seeking to unwrap the mystery of El Dorado. Some insist that a golden city lies hidden in the grasp of the rain forest. Others think that the forbidden Lake Guatavita holds treasures that may never be uncovered. Skeptics say that El Dorado is a myth—nothing more.

[33]Perhaps we'll never know if El Dorado really existed. But the search for golden dreams can often be as fascinating as the discovery.

If you have been timing your reading speed for this story, record your time below.

_____ : _____

Minutes   *Seconds*

Can You Believe This?

UNDERSTANDING THE MAIN IDEA

The following questions will demonstrate your understanding of what the story is about, or the *main idea*. Choose the best answer for each question.

1. This story is mainly about

Ⓐ an ancient gold lake.

Ⓑ the seven cities of gold.

Ⓒ the legend of "El Dorado."

Ⓓ the Spanish conquest in the Americas.

2. This story could have been titled

Ⓐ "A Mysterious Legend."

Ⓑ "The Gold Touch."

Ⓒ "Columbus's Folly."

Ⓓ "Happiness in the Rain Forest."

3. Which detail best supports the main idea of the story?

Ⓐ An ancient ceremony featured a man covered in gold dust diving into a lake.

Ⓑ By mistake, Columbus called the natives *Indians*.

Ⓒ The conquistadors forced 4,000 Indians to go with them and act as guides.

Ⓓ Mosquitoes spread a deadly disease—malaria.

4. Find another detail that supports the main idea of this story. Write it on the lines below.

_____

_____

RECALLING FACTS

The following questions will test how well you remember the facts in the story you just read. Choose the best answer for each question.

1. *El Dorado* is Spanish for

Ⓐ "The Lake in the Sky."

Ⓑ "The Golden Man."

Ⓒ "The Evil One."

Ⓓ "The Red Woman."

2. Lake Guatavita may have been the site of

Ⓐ a huge gold mine.

Ⓑ Gonzalo Pizarro's death at the hands of his followers.

Ⓒ a bloody massacre of native villagers.

Ⓓ a religious ceremony featuring gold sacrifices.

3. Francisco de Orellana and his party never returned with food for Gonzalo Pizarro and his men because

Ⓐ they didn't want to share the food.

Ⓑ they were killed by hostile natives.

Ⓒ the current was too strong.

Ⓓ they didn't know where to find Pizarro and his men.

4. Gonzalo Pizarro and his men

Ⓐ never found El Dorado.

Ⓑ discovered El Dorado, but then couldn't find it again.

Ⓒ found El Dorado, but all the gold was gone.

Ⓓ died in El Dorado.

READING BETWEEN THE LINES

An *inference* is a conclusion drawn from facts. A *generalization* is a general statement, idea, or rule that is supported by facts. Analyze the story by choosing the best answer to each question below.

1. **What conclusion can you draw from paragraph 9?**

   Ⓐ Natives were able to use their gold to buy more valuable European goods.

   Ⓑ Gold was not as important to the natives as it was to Europeans.

   Ⓒ Natives had never seen gold before the Europeans arrived.

   Ⓓ The natives preferred silver to gold.

2. **What conclusion can you draw from paragraph 14?**

   Ⓐ Natives were always treated fairly by Europeans.

   Ⓑ The natives were willing to help Pizarro.

   Ⓒ The natives knew where El Dorado was.

   Ⓓ Pizarro did not treat the natives with respect.

3. **What generalization can you make from the story?**

   Ⓐ Gold is more valuable than any person's life.

   Ⓑ Many people were willing to risk a lot for gold.

   Ⓒ All Spanish conquistadors treated the natives well.

   Ⓓ No Native Americans wanted to help the Europeans.

4. **It can be inferred from the story that**

   Ⓐ no one knows for sure if El Dorado was real or where it was.

   Ⓑ the Colombian government is hiding El Dorado.

   Ⓒ there is no gold left in the Andes.

   Ⓓ the Colombian natives were not religious.

Can You Believe This?

DETERMINING CAUSE AND EFFECT

Choose the best answers for the following questions to show the relationship between what happened in the story (*effects*) and why those things happened (*causes*).

1. Because Christopher Columbus thought he was near India, he

Ⓐ gave his followers the wrong directions.

Ⓑ quit his exploration.

Ⓒ called the natives *Indians*.

Ⓓ never went back to Spain.

2. What happened because Christopher Columbus took gold back to Spain?

Ⓐ He was robbed.

Ⓑ He was forbidden to return to the New World.

Ⓒ Europeans thought the New World was full of gold.

Ⓓ He lived in a very expensive house.

3. Why did Gonzalo Pizarro and his men go into the rain forest?

Ⓐ The king wanted them to make a map of the area.

Ⓑ They wanted to find a city of gold.

Ⓒ They were trying to escape hostile Native Americans.

Ⓓ They wanted to make friends with the tribes living there.

4. Why did villagers tell Gonzalo Pizarro's men a city of gold was close by?

Ⓐ They were trying to hide the location of the real El Dorado.

Ⓑ They misunderstood what Pizarro wanted.

Ⓒ They really believed the city was there.

Ⓓ They wanted to get rid of the soldiers.

USING CONTEXT CLUES

Skilled readers often find the meaning of unfamiliar words by using *context clues*. This means they study the way the words are used in the text. Use the context clues in the excerpts below to determine the meaning of each **bold-faced** word. Then choose the answer that best matches the meaning of the word.

1. "The **gilded** chief sat on a throne that was placed upon a raft." (paragraph 3)

Write what you think the **bold-faced** word means. Then record the context clues that led you to this definition.

Meaning:

_____

_____

_____

Context clues:

_____

_____

_____

2. "They [Pizarro and his men] heard that El Dorado was a kingdom hidden in the **unchartered** rain forest, east of Quito."

CLUE: "Indians used machetes to hack a trail through thick tangles of plants and trees."

  Ⓐ wet

  Ⓑ wild

  Ⓒ sparse

  Ⓓ rich

3. "After leaving the mountainous town of Quito, the long **caravan** wound down into the rain forest."

CLUE: "The conquistadors forced 4,000 Indians to go with them. . . They loaded heavy baggage on the backs of hundreds of llamas. For food, 4,000 pigs were taken along."

  Ⓐ group

  Ⓑ bridge

  Ⓒ road

  Ⓓ wagons

4. "When **skirmishes** broke out, soldiers fired their muskets and crossbows."

CLUE: "Some villagers fiercely resisted the Europeans."

  Ⓐ diseases

  Ⓑ prisoners

  Ⓒ fights

  Ⓓ parties

End-of-Unit Activities

1. The name of this unit is "Secrets of the Past." Why do we find past secrets and mysteries fascinating? To answer that question, determine what characteristics all the stories in each of the four lessons in this unit have in common. List at least five similarities below. Then think of two "secrets" or mysteries from your lifetime that you think future students will see as intriguing "secrets of the past." The secrets should have the same characteristics that you came up with for the stories in this unit.

Want to Find Lost Treasures?

Do Cannibals and Headhunters Exist?

Who or What Is El Dorado?

Why Do Egyptian Mummies Fascinate Us?

Similarities

_____

_____

_____

_____

_____

_____

_____

_____

_____

Future "Secrets of the Past"

_____

_____

_____

_____

End-of-Unit Activities

2. **Rank each of the stories in this unit, from the one you liked the most to the one you liked the least. For each story, write one interesting fact you learned. Then write a paragraph describing why you liked the story you ranked *1* the best.**

LESSON 5 Ranking _____

_____

_____

_____

LESSON 6 Ranking _____

_____

_____

_____

LESSON 7 Ranking _____

_____

_____

_____

LESSON 8 Ranking _____

_____

_____

_____

Why did you like the story you ranked *1* the best?

_____

_____

_____

_____

_____

Words-Per-Minute Chart

Directions:

Use the chart to find your words-per-minute reading speed. Refer to the reading time you recorded at the end of each article. Find your reading time in seconds along the left-hand side of the chart or minutes and seconds along the right-hand side of the chart. Your words-per-minute score will be listed next to the time in the column below the appropriate lesson number.

No. of Words	Lesson 5 1656	Lesson 6 1509	Lesson 7 1607	Lesson 8 1583	Minutes and Seconds
80	1242	1132	1205	1187	1:20
100	994	905	964	950	1:40
120	828	755	804	792	2:00
140	710	647	689	678	2:20
160	621	566	603	594	2:40
180	552	503	536	528	3:00
200	497	453	482	475	3:20
220	452	412	438	432	3:40
240	414	377	402	396	4:00
260	382	348	371	365	4:20
280	355	323	344	339	4:40
300	331	302	321	317	5:00
320	311	283	301	297	5:20
340	292	266	284	279	5:40
360	276	252	268	264	6:00
380	261	238	254	250	6:20
400	248	226	241	237	6:40
420	237	216	230	226	7:00
440	226	206	219	216	7:20
460	216	197	210	206	7:40
480	207	189	201	198	8:00
500	199	181	193	190	8:20
520	191	174	185	183	8:40
540	184	168	179	176	9:00
560	177	162	172	170	9:20
580	171	156	166	164	9:40
600	166	151	161	158	10:00
620	160	146	156	153	10:20
640	155	141	151	148	10:40
660	151	137	146	144	11:00
680	146	133	142	140	11:20
700	142	129	138	136	11:40
720	138	126	134	132	12:00
740	134	122	130	128	12:20
760	131	119	127	125	12:40
780	127	116	124	122	13:00
800	124	113	121	119	13:20
820	121	110	118	116	13:40
840	118	108	115	113	14:00

Seconds (left-hand side label) · Minutes and Seconds (right-hand side label)

UNIT THREE—
freaks of nature

What Is Lightning?

Every second, nearly 100 bolts of lightning strike our planet. In a 24-hour day, that adds up to 10 million bolts that hit in various places around the world.

[2] A bolt of lightning is only about an inch around. It seems bigger because of the brilliant light given off by its 50,000 degree Fahrenheit temperature. The sizzling heat is five times hotter than the surface of the sun! Most lightning bolts measure three or four miles in length. But some bolts stretch a whopping ten miles.

[3] Lightning puts on a dazzling show during a thunderstorm. Radiant ribbons of light etch zigzag trails across the sky. But what causes lightning? How dangerous is it? Can we find a way to use its power? Questions like this have fascinated people for many years.

[4] It was 1752 in Philadelphia, Pennsylvania. Low rumbles of thunder announced an approaching late spring storm. One of the most famous American colonists,

Benjamin Franklin, was excited. He said to himself, "A big storm is brewing. Today is the day!"

[5] People did not have electricity at this time. But a few scientists had experimented with it by creating sparks in their labs. Like other scientists, Franklin believed that lightning was electricity. He had a chance to prove it that day.

[6] Franklin prepared to fly a kite made of silk fabric stretched over a lightweight wooden frame. A metal wire stuck up from the top of the frame. A long string hung from the bottom of the kite. At the loose end of the string, Franklin tied a large metal key, then attached a silk ribbon. He held on to the silk ribbon as the kite soared skyward in the gusty winds and rain.

[7] Ben Franklin could have been killed during this experiment. Luckily, his kite was not zapped by

a direct hit. When lightning flashed nearby, the wet string carried the voltage to the key, and sparks jumped. Franklin smiled—satisfied that lightning was indeed electricity.

[8]A safer experiment can be done inside. When the air is dry, drag your shoes on a carpet, then touch a metal doorknob. Watch for sparks, and feel the mild jolt. You've made a tiny bolt of lightning.

[9]Today we know much more about lightning than anyone knew during Franklin's time. However, we're still learning. Scientists called *meteorologists* study weather conditions. They warn us when storms are near. A beautiful morning of sunshine can turn into an afternoon hit by a violent thunderstorm.

[10]The warm day starts with a blazing sun on a backdrop of blue sky. In the afternoon, changes begin. Moisture from the ground rises in the warm air. As it flows upward, the humid air cools, forming puffy white clouds. The sky becomes spotted with cotton balls called *cumulus* clouds. The cumulus clouds drift together, then combine. More warm air is sucked up into the steadily growing clouds.

[11]The top of the thick cloud soon reaches high enough to touch the coldness of the high atmosphere. At this stage, the cloud can tower over 6 miles high. Drops of water and ice form inside the mass. The huge cloud darkens. Now it is a *cumulonimbus*. The top of the cloud flattens into an anvil-shaped thunderhead. Hail, then rain, pelts the earth.

[12]Inside the mushrooming thunderhead, turbulence builds. Winds blow and pieces of ice crystals collide. The activity within grows more frenzied as rising warm air meets sinking cold air. Moving at speeds more than 100 miles per hour, the churning winds cause positive charges to build at the top of the cloud, while negative charges form at the bottom.

[13]Then it happens. The charges explode into an electrical spark. A flash of lightning erupts as electricity leaps from the top to the bottom of the cloud. The reflected light inside the cloud is seen from the ground as *intracloud lightning*. Most of the lightning during a thunderstorm is this type. The dark cloud brightens and flickers. Distant muffled thunder might be heard. If lightning travels between two different clouds, it's called *cloud-to-cloud lightning*. But we are most familiar with the third type, *cloud-to-earth lightning*. It grabs our attention.

[14]Suddenly, a lightning bolt slices toward the ground. While charges were building within a thunderhead, the ground below the cloud was also becoming electrically charged. From the bottom of the dark cloud a negative charge plunges down to meet a positive charge shooting up from the ground. Their jagged paths form a channel for a return stroke of lightning that branches across the sky. The brief flash can be as bright as a million 100-watt light bulbs. For an instant, its power is equal to all of the electricity-generating plants in the United States.

[15]Thunder follows the flash. A lightning bolt superheats the air around it. The air quickly expands, making shock waves—thunder. Light from a bolt reaches your eyes almost instantly. Sound waves are slower. It takes five seconds for the sound waves of thunder to travel one mile. As soon as you see lightning, count the seconds until you hear thunder to determine the distance of the storm.

[16]A storm that is approaching or leaving rumbles and rolls. When lightning flashes far away, the expanding air's sound waves reach your ears at different times. The rumbling is the merging of the sounds. When a violent storm is directly overhead, you hear loud cracks of thunder with the flashes.

[17]Although thunder scares us with earsplitting noises, the danger comes from lightning. Forest fires can be started by lightning strikes. Sometimes the fires are nature's way of cleaning the forest, allowing new plants and trees to grow. Out of control, though, forest fires destroy property and threaten lives.

[18]Lightning can also be a ruthless killer. Each year about 130 people in the United States die from lightning strikes. Over 1,000 other people are struck, but survive.

[19]Long ago, lightning was a mystery to people. Some people thought that lightning was magic. Ancient stories were told to explain the zigzag patterns in the sky and the booming noises. One tale described a giant bird's flight. Its wings flapped, causing thunder, while lightning flashed from the bird's feathers. Others believed that during storms, angry gods threw thunderbolts at Earth.

[20]Even with today's knowledge, we find it awesome to witness the force of a violent thunderstorm. It's fascinating to watch the storm from a safe place. Drenching rain pounds the earth. Crooked streaks of neon light snake across the dark sky.

Can You Believe This?

Benjamin Franklin

Thunder crashes and echoes overhead. The show is spectacular.

[21]Scientists continue to study lightning. They have much to learn. Perhaps one day we will be able to capture the power of a lightning flash. Millions of volts of electricity could be put to use. Think of the possibilities.

If you have been timing your reading speed for this story, record your time below.

_____ : _____

Minutes   Seconds

UNDERSTANDING THE MAIN IDEA

The following questions will demonstrate your understanding of what the story is about, or the *main idea*. Choose the best answer for each question.

1. This story is mainly about

Ⓐ people who are hit by lightning.

Ⓑ what causes lightning.

Ⓒ the time lapse between lightning and thunder.

Ⓓ how to make lightning.

2. This story could have been titled

Ⓐ "Lightning Is Electric!"

Ⓑ "Ben's Kite."

Ⓒ "The Flash of Thunder."

Ⓓ "In the Eye of a Hurricane."

3. Which detail best supports the main idea of the story?

Ⓐ People did not have electricity in 1752.

Ⓑ Franklin was satisfied that lightning is electricity.

Ⓒ The warm day starts with a blazing sun in a blue sky.

Ⓓ Winds blow and pieces of ice crystals collide.

4. Find another detail that supports the main idea of this story. Write it on the lines below.

_____

_____

RECALLING FACTS

The following questions will test how well you remember the facts in the story you just read. Choose the best answer for each question.

1. A bolt of lightning is about

Ⓐ 1 inch around.

Ⓑ 8 inches around.

Ⓒ 12 inches around.

Ⓓ 2 feet around.

2. Ben Franklin proved that lightning is electricity by using a silk kite with a wire and a

Ⓐ phone.

Ⓑ hook.

Ⓒ key.

Ⓓ lamp.

3. Lightning is caused when positive and negative charges

Ⓐ drift apart.

Ⓑ move.

Ⓒ repel each other.

Ⓓ explode.

4. Thunder comes from

Ⓐ clouds colliding.

Ⓑ air that is superheated by lightning.

Ⓒ bowling tournaments held by the gods.

Ⓓ two storms hitting each other.

Can You Believe This?

READING BETWEEN THE LINES

An *inference* is a conclusion drawn from facts. A *generalization* is a general statement, idea, or rule that is supported by facts. Analyze the story by choosing the best answer to each question below.

1. What conclusion can you draw from paragraphs 4–5?

Ⓐ Franklin loved big thunderstorms.

Ⓑ Franklin wanted to experiment with lightning.

Ⓒ Franklin was frightened by lightning.

Ⓓ Franklin had never heard of electricity.

2. What conclusion can you draw from paragraph 7?

Ⓐ Lightning can be very dangerous.

Ⓑ Franklin knew lightning would not hit the kite.

Ⓒ Franklin had hoped to be hit by lightning.

Ⓓ Franklin didn't think lightning was electricity.

3. What generalization about lightning can you make from the story? Answer on the lines below, using complete sentences.

_____

_____

_____

_____

_____

_____

4. It can be inferred from the story that

Ⓐ there are still many questions about lightning.

Ⓑ no one knows what causes lightning.

Ⓒ scientists are learning how to make lightning.

Ⓓ scientists have found a way to stop lightning.

———————

DETERMINING CAUSE AND EFFECT

Choose the best answers for the following questions to show the relationship between what happened in the story (*effects*) and why those things happened (*causes*).

1. **Because Ben Franklin thought lightning was electricity, he**

   Ⓐ presented many papers about it.

   Ⓑ told people that electricity could kill them.

   Ⓒ experimented with a kite in a storm.

   Ⓓ hated thunderstorms.

2. **What happens because humid air rises?**

   Ⓐ It's always cold and dry close to the ground.

   Ⓑ The air cools and forms clouds.

   Ⓒ Moisture from the ground rises.

   Ⓓ It never rains.

3. **Why does the air around a lightning bolt expand?**

   Ⓐ The air is cooled by the lightning.

   Ⓑ The lightning creates a hole in the atmosphere.

   Ⓒ No one really knows.

   Ⓓ The air is heated by the lightning.

4. **Why did some people long ago think lightning was magic?**

   Ⓐ Wizards used lightning in their spells.

   Ⓑ They didn't know what caused lightning.

   Ⓒ Flowers always bloomed after a lightning strike.

   Ⓓ Lightning always struck in the same place.

USING CONTEXT CLUES

Skilled readers often find the meaning of unfamiliar words by using *context clues*. This means they study the way the words are used in the text. Use the context clues in the excerpts below to determine the meaning of each **bold-faced** word. Then choose the answer that best matches the meaning of the word.

1. "Every **second**, nearly 100 bolts of lightning strike our planet."

CLUE: "In a 24-hour day, that adds up to 10 million bolts that hit in various places around the world."

   Ⓐ place after first

   Ⓑ another helping

   Ⓒ 1/60 of a minute

   Ⓓ moment

2. "**Radiant** ribbons of light etch zigzag trails across the sky."

CLUE: "Lightning puts on a dazzling show during a thunderstorm."

   Ⓐ Bright

   Ⓑ Long

   Ⓒ Narrow

   Ⓓ Straight

3. "As it flows upward, the **humid** air cools, forming puffy white clouds."

CLUE: "Moisture from the ground rises in the warm air."

   Ⓐ dry

   Ⓑ heavy

   Ⓒ wet

   Ⓓ blue

4. "Inside the mushrooming thunderhead, **turbulence** builds."

CLUE: "Winds blow and pieces of ice crystals collide."

   Ⓐ peace

   Ⓑ motion

   Ⓒ water

   Ⓓ heat

Must We Sleep?

O ur lives are hectic. There aren't enough hours in a day. "Life is too short," we complain.

[2]Think of all of the time we lose. Sleep takes up about one-third of each 24 hours. A 90-year-old person has slept away 30 years of his or her lifetime. What is this thing called "sleep" that steals a third of our lives?

[3]Scientists wonder too. In a research investigation, they kept rats awake day and night. After an average of 16 days without sleep, a curious thing happened. The rats died. Scientists examined each rat to determine the cause of death. What did they find? Nothing. Autopsies showed that the internal organs of the rats appeared normal. Yet they died.

[4]The rats ate twice as much as usual during the experiment, but they still lost 20% of their body weight. Toward the end, the rats' body temperatures dropped. This suggests that lack of sleep triggered overactive metabolic rates. Without sleep, normal body temperatures could not be maintained.

[5]In another research project, rats that were not permitted to sleep developed blood infections. Their immune systems refused to function properly.

[6]Would humans react like the rats? Scientific tests with humans are not pushed to the dangerous level of the rat experiments. But there have been some documented cases of people who stayed awake for long periods of time. Each person displayed behavior as that of a young man named Randy Gardner. Gardner had no sleep for 11 days (264 hours). Here's what happened to him.

[7]On Day 1, nothing unusual happened. On Day 2, he had difficulty focusing his eyes. He stopped watching television. By Day 3 he had become moody. His physical strength and coordination had declined.

Can You Believe This?

[8]On Day 4, Gardner was cranky and negative. He suffered from memory lapses and was unable to concentrate. He experienced his first hallucination. On Days 5 and 6, he had more hallucinations and developed muscular weakness. His speech slowed, and he had difficulty naming common objects.

[9]By Days 7 and 8, his speech was slurred. He was noticeably irritable. He had more difficulty with memory and concentration. On Days 9 and 10 his vision became blurred. He did not finish sentences. Paranoia, the state of being suspicious and distrustful of others, began to set in.

[10]By Day 11, he had a short attention span. He suffered muscle tremors in his fingers. His eyes were unfocused. His speech was slurred, and he was reluctant to talk at all. His mental abilities were also greatly reduced.

[11]After this experiment, Gardner slept for nearly 15 hours. He then returned to normal, both mentally and physically. '

[12]Okay, so we can't do without sleep, but can we at least sleep less? Some people try to cut back on the number of hours they slumber each night. Their bodies do not cooperate. The missed hours of sleep keep adding up until the individual "crashes." It takes a catch-up night of extra hours of sleep to recharge the person's energy level.

[13]Why do we get tired—what is sleep's purpose? Sleep researchers admit they can't pinpoint exact reasons, but they offer theories about why we need to sleep.

[14]Rat experiments showed that sleep helps control body temperature and boost the immune system. Some scientists think that sleep also keeps the brain's chemical balance in check. It's a renewal time to meet the demands of waking hours. In scattered areas of the brain, activity slows or shuts down during sleep. Muscles relax, the heartbeat slows, and blood pressure falls.

[15]Perhaps this is the time the brain processes information and memories. Each day our brain overloads on data. While we sleep, certain parts of the brain swing into action, working the "night shift." The brain sorts experiences and stores important details. Like an updated file, the brain is now ready for a new day of mental alertness.

[16]Human babies snooze a total of 18 or more hours each day. Toddlers sleep 10 to 12 hours, plus nap once or twice. Older children get about

ten hours of nightly sleep. By the time we become teenagers and adults, we sleep an average of seven or eight hours each night. Is this long enough? If we had no clocks, no schedules, and no appointments to keep, how would our bodies respond?

[17]Volunteers took part in studies to learn if our bodies have internal clocks. Outside influences were removed. The people lived in underground labs, isolated and unaware of daylight or darkness. No clocks ticked the time. Volunteers soon adjusted to a daily routine about 25 hours long. They had a main period of sleep and added a short nap midway through their waking hours.

[18]A surprising outcome of these studies was that the adult subjects tended to sleep longer—a total of nine or ten hours. This suggests that teens and adults need more sleep than their usual seven or eight hours each night.

[19]We don't know exactly why we sleep, but do we know what happens during sleep? Sleep researchers try to find out. They use a machine called an EEG (electroencephalograph) to measure brain waves and record them on a graph. When the person is awake, the waves are short and fast. Then

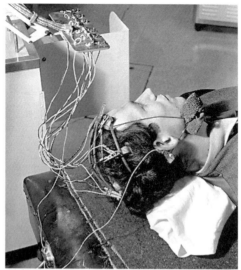

Taking an EEG of the brain

the patterns slow down as the volunteer falls asleep. Very slow waves appear when a deep sleep is reached.

[20]About every 90 to 100 minutes during sleep, the brain sends out shorter and faster waves again. The sleeper is not awake but is undergoing rapid eye movement— REM sleep. Eyes are closed, but they move quickly back and forth. This is when dreams take place. The person's mind creates stories out of past experiences.

[21]Even animals have REM sleep. Watch a dog or a cat in this stage of sleep. Maybe you'll see legs twitching as if it's dreaming about running.

Can You Believe This?

[22]Most people have about four REM periods a night, each lasting between 5 and 15 minutes. Dreams most likely to be remembered are those taking place during the last REM period before waking.

[23]Not all dreams are remembered, but they must be important. If volunteers in sleep labs are awakened each time they start to dream, they feel grouchy and groggy the next day.

[24]Sleep disorders bother some people. Sleepwalking or sleeptalking occurs when areas of the brain remain active at a time that they should be shut down. Another disorder is insomnia—the person is unable to sleep. The opposite of this is narcolepsy. People with this condition have "sleep attacks." They often fall asleep while talking, walking, or eating.

[25]Future research might lift the layers of mystery regarding sleep. For now, much about sleep stumps us. Even trying to catch the instant you fall asleep is impossible. As you relax, it may feel like you are slowly drifting to sleep. But when you actually fall asleep, you simply sink into blankness. Your awareness just switches off. In reverse, when you awaken, your awareness switches on.

[26]Are you an early bird or a night owl? Most of us fit into one of these categories. An early bird, or "lark," is alert in the morning, fades in the evening, and goes to sleep early. Night owls are groggy in the morning. They come alive in the afternoon or evening and like to stay up late. Recent research points to a human gene that might control the sleep cycle.

[27]Whichever way we function, as an owl or a lark, we've not persuaded our bodies to give us more time awake. Improved health care and diets have extended our average life spans. However, we've not discovered a way to sleep less. One-third of our lifetime is spent sleeping, and sleep does not appear to be optional. Our bodies demand it.

If you have been timing your reading speed for this story, record your time below.

_____ : _____

Minutes   **Seconds**

UNDERSTANDING THE MAIN IDEA

The following questions will demonstrate your understanding of what the story is about, or the *main idea*. Choose the best answer for each question.

1. This story is mainly about

Ⓐ family duties today.

Ⓑ the meaning of dreams.

Ⓒ our bodies' need for sleep.

Ⓓ rats in science experiments about sleep.

2. This story could have been titled

Ⓐ "You Snooze, You Lose."

Ⓑ "The Need to Sleep."

Ⓒ "Tired Rats."

Ⓓ "Dreaming About Our Lives."

3. Which detail best supports the main idea of the story?

Ⓐ Scientists kept rats awake day and night.

Ⓑ Autopsies showed that the rats appeared normal.

Ⓒ Randy Gardner was cranky on Day 4.

Ⓓ Researchers have theories about why we need to sleep.

4. Find another detail that supports the main idea of the story. Write it on the lines below.

_____

_____

RECALLING FACTS

The following questions will test how well you remember the facts in the story you just read. Choose the best answer for each question.

1. After about 16 days without sleep, rats in experiments

Ⓐ fell asleep.

Ⓑ died.

Ⓒ stopped eating.

Ⓓ escaped their cages.

2. Randy Gardner had no sleep for

Ⓐ 11 days.

Ⓑ 12 weeks.

Ⓒ 1 month.

Ⓓ 2 years.

3. During sleep, brain activity

Ⓐ speeds up.

Ⓑ slows down.

Ⓒ stops then starts again.

Ⓓ stops completely.

4. Dreams happen during

Ⓐ the first part of sleep.

Ⓑ stressful sleep experiments.

Ⓒ cold nights.

Ⓓ REM sleep.

——— ▬ ———

Can You Believe This?

An *inference* is a conclusion drawn from facts. A *generalization* is a general statement, idea, or rule that is supported by facts. Analyze the story by choosing the best answer to each question below.

1. What conclusion can you draw from paragraphs 6–11?

Ⓐ Gardner didn't need as much sleep as other people.

Ⓑ Gardner wasn't allowed to sleep because of his job.

Ⓒ Gardner's body needed sleep to function properly.

Ⓓ Gardner never completely recovered from his experiment.

2. What conclusion can you draw from paragraph 17?

Ⓐ It's impossible to sleep without knowing whether it's day or night.

Ⓑ People automatically adjust to regular day and night routines.

Ⓒ People should take naps at midday.

Ⓓ We should change our clocks so we have 25-hour days.

3. What generalization can you make from the story?

Ⓐ Most people need several hours of sleep each day.

Ⓑ Almost everyone gets too much sleep.

Ⓒ No one should sleep more than 3 hours each day.

Ⓓ Most people dream about the future.

4. It can be inferred from the story that

Ⓐ people often live without any sleep.

Ⓑ if you go without sleep for two days, you'll get a blood infection.

Ⓒ sleep is needed for our bodies to work correctly.

Ⓓ sleep disorders are extremely rare.

DETERMINING CAUSE AND EFFECT

Choose the best answers for the following questions to show the relationship between what happened in the story (*effects*) and why those things happened (*causes*).

1. Because scientists wondered why people need sleep, the scientists

Ⓐ stayed awake as long as they could.

Ⓑ studied people who had trouble sleeping.

Ⓒ kept people awake for two months.

Ⓓ kept rats awake for 16 days.

2. What happened because Randy Gardner went without sleep for many days?

Ⓐ He learned to manage without sleeping ever again.

Ⓑ He lost most of his body weight.

Ⓒ He suffered several physical and mental problems.

Ⓓ He slept for 11 straight days after the experiment.

3. Why do some scientists think adults need more than eight hours of sleep?

Ⓐ An experiment showed that adults naturally sleep nine to ten hours.

Ⓑ It's dark outside longer than eight hours.

Ⓒ Volunteers fall asleep after being awake 14 hours.

Ⓓ Babies sleep 18 hours a day.

4. Why do people need sleep? Write your answer on the lines below, using complete sentences.

_____

_____

_____

_____

_____

_____

Can You Believe This?

USING CONTEXT CLUES

Skilled readers often find the meaning of unfamiliar words by using *context clues*. This means they study the way the words are used in the text. Use the context clues in the excerpts below to determine the meaning of each **bold-faced** word. Then choose the answer that best matches the meaning of the word.

1. "**Autopsies** showed that the internal organs of the rats appeared normal."

CLUE: "Scientists examined each rat to determine the cause of death."

Ⓐ Questions

Ⓑ Tests

Ⓒ Burials

Ⓓ Doctors

2. ". . . [T]here have been some **documented** cases of people who stayed awake for long periods of time."

CLUE: "Scientific tests with humans are not pushed to the dangerous level of the rat experiments."

Ⓐ recorded

Ⓑ unproven

Ⓒ severe

Ⓓ unknown

3. "Sleep researchers admit they can't pinpoint exact reasons, but they offer **theories** about why we need to sleep."

CLUE: "Why do we get tired—what is sleep's purpose?"

Ⓐ science

Ⓑ papers

Ⓒ ideas

Ⓓ proof

4. "Outside **influences** were removed."

CLUE: "The people lived in underground labs, isolated and unaware of daylight or darkness."

Ⓐ factors

Ⓑ weather

Ⓒ shoes

Ⓓ houses

Who's Afraid of the Big, Bad Wolverine?

Two hikers trudged through the Alaskan wilderness. The men did not see the pair of eyes watching them.

[2]Nearby, in the underbrush, a wolverine had stirred from a four-hour nap. It caught the scent of the approaching men when they were hundreds of yards away. The wolverine's instincts told it to either run away or stay hidden and be wary of these two-legged creatures.

[3]One of the hikers stopped. "What's that smell?" Sniffing deeply, the other man said, "Yikes! It's worse than a skunk, whatever it is. Let's get out of here!" They hurried on.

[4]The men were unaware that they were close to one of the most elusive mammals in North America. It is rare for people to see a wolverine in the wild. That makes it difficult to know much about this animal with a nasty-tempered reputation.

[5]Satisfied that the intruders were gone, the wolverine ambled to a hidden storage spot, or cache. It began to dig in the dirt and rocks, using muscular paws armed with inch-long claws. Soon a half-eaten deer carcass was uncovered, reeking with a foul odor. Earlier, the wolverine had used special glands to spray a urinelike substance over the leftovers. The repulsive stench curbed the appetites of other scavengers, discouraging them from stealing the carcass.

[6]Loud snapping sounds broke the stillness of the air. The hungry wolverine's powerful jaws and sharp teeth splintered the thick bones of the deer. This bone-crushing ability is why the species is called the "hyena of the North." After gorging until its belly was full, the wolverine slept again. Then the cycle would be repeated—look for food, eat, sleep.

[7]The big, bad wolverine is actually not very big. Related to the weasel, the wolverine looks more like a small bear. Some Native American tribes named it the "skunk bear" because of,

Can You Believe This?

yes—its stinky spray!

[8]The average length of a wolverine is 3 feet, including an 8-inch-long furry tail. The animal stands about 16 inches high at the shoulders and weighs about 35 pounds. It may be small, but pound for pound, this critter is one of the fiercest competitors in the wilderness.

[9]A wolverine wears a long, heavy coat of fur—usually a dark brown color. Two bands of lighter-colored hair run along the sides of the stocky body, from the shoulders to the tail.

[10]The sparsely scattered animals prefer cold northern climates. Small populations live in a few of the connected 48 states, mostly in the Northwest and in the Rocky Mountains. But the largest numbers are found throughout Alaska and wide areas of Canada.

[11]Wolverines are solitary animals. Each requires a large territory of about 500 square miles. No wonder they are hard to find! They mark their territories with smelly spray, warning other wolverines to stay out!

[12]The wolverine's scientific name is *Gulo gulo,* which means "glutton." This name was earned by the greedy manner in which it tears into food.

[13]Don't get between a wolverine and a meal! Bigger predators, like cougars, wolves, and some bears, have had kills stolen from them by a growling, snarling wolverine. It's an aggressive, ferocious fighter. That's why it collects more nicknames like "devil bear" and "evil one."

[14]Many times the wolverine only needs to bluff its way out of situations. Not many animals will tangle with the fearless creature. Grizzly bears and wolf packs are about the only other predators that will kill a wolverine.

[15]The wolverine's main enemy, however, is man. Trappers consider the animal's fur valuable because the hairs repel ice crystals. Frost and frozen breath do not cling to the fur, so it's valued for lining hoods on snow jackets. Many people want laws to protect wolverines from being killed for their pelts.

[16]Trappers have found reasons to dislike wolverines. Often, the intelligent animals avoid traps but cleverly steal the bait. To further annoy trappers, wolverines brazenly eat other animals caught by the traps, for an easy "fast-food" meal.

[17]Wolverines usually avoid humans, but occasionally the rascals break into remote cabins and help themselves to food. Here's what happened when a wolverine stumbled upon an isolated cabin.

[18]The wolverine's sensitive nose smelled food. It also recognized the scents of humans. The animal circled the wooden cabin until it was certain that no one was around. Finding a small hole in a wall, the wolverine enlarged the hole by tearing off chunks of wood with its strong forepaws. Then it squeezed inside.

[19]Like a furry tornado, the wolverine left a trail of destruction throughout the cabin. Shelves crashed to the floor, shattering bottles and dishes. Cans of food were pierced by sharp teeth. Boxes and bags were ripped open. Sugar and flour blanketed the floor like powdery snow.

[20]Across the white mess, footprints identified the guilty culprit. Each print measured 4 inches wide by 5 inches long. Five toes on each oversized foot proved that a wolverine had stopped by for a visit and a snack.

[21]A wolverine's keen sense of smell makes up for poor eyesight. Its nose leads it to sites where other predators have hidden their kills. As a scavenger, it devours carrion. A wolverine is not picky. It eats just about anything it can find. Although a scavenger much of the time, a wolverine will hunt when necessary.

[22]As a hunter, the wolverine's loping run of about 20 miles per hour isn't fast enough to catch large prey. In the summertime it manages to catch and eat small animals like rodents, birds, snakes, or frogs. The summer menu might also include roots, berries, eggs, and insects. A special treat is bee larvae. The stings of enraged bees do not intimidate the thick-coated wolverine.

[23]In the winter the wolverine hunts with an advantage. Broad furry paws become built-in snowshoes. It zooms across the top of the snow, while animals with hooves flounder in deep snowdrifts. That's when a wolverine can outrun and kill deer, elk, or even a moose—especially old or weak animals. The wolverine brings down the victim by biting it on the throat. Its vicious jaws clamp down with a viselike grip.

[24]One wolverine was observed crossing a field, towing a dead elk that was at least three times heavier than its own weight. With its incredible strength, the wolverine was able to drag the elk for more than a mile.

[25]Endurance is another trait that adds to the wolverine's reputation. It covers its huge territory by jogging with a rocking-horse gait. Mile after mile, the tireless animal bounds on short legs without resting.

[26]Trackers once followed a wolverine for 40 miles. Without

stopping, they trailed through fields, through woods, and over hills. When a river appeared, the wolverine easily swam across the water and loped out of sight from weary pursuers. Stories like this add to its fame as a tough and determined creature.

[27]If wolverines are so strong and clever, why are there so few of them? Unfortunately, humans have crowded the animals out of areas by building new highways, houses, factories, and towns. Farmers and ranchers trap, poison, and shoot wolverines when they kill livestock. And wolverines have a low birth rate.

[28]We don't know a lot about their mating habits. We believe that a female wolverine delivers between two and four babies, called *kits*. They stay with their mother for about seven months. Then they split up to find their own territories. It is thought that many kits do not survive the first year alone in the harsh wilderness. Survivors *might* live about ten years.

[29]Since wolverines are hard to find and study, there's much we do not know about them. How far do they travel each day? Are they more social with one another than we think? What is their true average life span? How many wolverines exist in the wild? Researchers fear that the elusive animals are becoming more scarce each year. They could already be an endangered species. We just don't know.

[30]Wolverines do not earn points for a likable personality. They deserve respect, though, for their feisty independence. Like other scavengers, they provide a useful cleanup service in the wilderness.

[31]Scientists want to livetrap wolverines, fit them with radio collars, and then release them. This could be the best way to learn more about the elusive animal's behavior. Meanwhile, with wolverines, our unanswered questions wait for answers.

If you have been timing your reading speed for this story, record your time below.

_____ : _____

Minutes   **Seconds**

UNDERSTANDING THE MAIN IDEA

The following questions will demonstrate your understanding of what the story is about, or the *main idea*. Choose the best answer for each question.

1. This story is mainly about

Ⓐ attacks on humans by wolverines.

Ⓑ the habits of wolverines.

Ⓒ hiking through Alaska.

Ⓓ a fierce wolverine that lives in South America.

2. This story could have been titled

Ⓐ "The Tropical Wolverine."

Ⓑ "Watch Out for That Wildcat!"

Ⓒ "Wolverine Eggs."

Ⓓ "The Elusive Wolverine."

3. Which detail best supports the main idea of the story?

Ⓐ The men were close to one of the most elusive mammals.

Ⓑ The two hikers stopped.

Ⓒ Each print measured 4 inches wide by 5 inches long.

Ⓓ The wolverine's scientific name is *Gulo gulo*, which means "glutton."

4. Find another detail that supports the main idea of this story. Write it on the lines below.

_____

_____

RECALLING FACTS

The following questions will test how well you remember the facts in the story you just read. Choose the best answer for each question.

1. The hikers could smell the wolverine because

Ⓐ it hadn't bathed in several days.

Ⓑ its den was full of rotten meat.

Ⓒ it had sprayed a smelly substance over its food.

Ⓓ the snow and cold made scents smell stronger.

2. On another sheet of paper, draw a picture of a wolverine as it's described in the text.

3. The wolverine's main enemies are

Ⓐ bears.

Ⓑ humans.

Ⓒ wolves.

Ⓓ cougars.

4. Wolverine fur is good for snow jackets because

Ⓐ it doesn't get wet.

Ⓑ it's such a pretty blue color.

Ⓒ it repels ice crystals.

Ⓓ it keeps wolverines warm in Canada.

READING BETWEEN THE LINES

An *inference* is a conclusion drawn from facts. A *generalization* is a general statement, idea, or rule that is supported by facts. Analyze the story by choosing the best answer to each question below.

1. What conclusion can you draw from paragraphs 13–14?

Ⓐ Many animals are frightened of wolverines.

Ⓑ Wolverines eat cougars and bears.

Ⓒ Wolverines hunt in packs.

Ⓓ Wolverines get very hungry.

2. What conclusion can you draw from paragraph 15?

Ⓐ More people are killed by wolverines each year.

Ⓑ Wolverines often escape from trappers.

Ⓒ More wolverines are killed by humans than by any other predator.

Ⓓ Wolverines are starting to take over human towns and cities.

3. What generalization can you make from the story?

Ⓐ All wolverines make good pets for children.

Ⓑ All people are frightened by wolverines.

Ⓒ Some wolverines have been found in Florida.

Ⓓ Most wolverines are fierce creatures.

4. It can be inferred from the story that

Ⓐ fewer wolverines are trapped each year.

Ⓑ it's hard to know how many wolverines there really are.

Ⓒ more and more wolverines are destroying homes.

Ⓓ wolverines die off in the cold winter months.

DETERMINING CAUSE AND EFFECT

Choose the best answers for the following questions to show the relationship between what happened in the story (*effects*) and why those things happened (*causes*).

1. **Because the wolverine didn't want other animals to eat its food, the wolverine**

    Ⓐ sprayed the food with a smelly substance.

    Ⓑ ate all the food at once.

    Ⓒ attacked the hikers.

    Ⓓ took turns guarding it with other wolverines.

2. **What happens because wolverines prefer to live alone in huge territories?**

    Ⓐ It's rare to see a wolverine in the wild.

    Ⓑ Wolverines build large fences.

    Ⓒ Wolverines eat berries and roots.

    Ⓓ It's usually easy to capture a wolverine.

3. **Why is it easier for wolverines to hunt in the winter?**

    Ⓐ There are more animals for them to hunt.

    Ⓑ The wolverines' paws can walk and run on top of the snow.

    Ⓒ The nights are longer, giving them more hours to hunt.

    Ⓓ The wolverines find more tracks to follow in the snow.

4. **Why don't people know much about wolverines?**

    Ⓐ Wolverines are hard to find and study.

    Ⓑ Wolverines are so mean, it's easier to leave them alone.

    Ⓒ Wolverines die almost immediately in captivity.

    Ⓓ Wolverines are an endangered species.

Can You Believe This?

USING CONTEXT CLUES

Skilled readers often find the meaning of unfamiliar words by using *context clues*. This means they study the way the words are used in the text. Use the context clues in the excerpts below to determine the meaning of each **bold-faced** word. Then choose the answer that best matches the meaning of the word.

1. "The men were unaware that they were close to one of the most **elusive** mammals in North America."

CLUE: "It is rare for people to see a wolverine in the wild."

   Ⓐ common

   Ⓑ colorful

   Ⓒ tame

   Ⓓ difficult to capture

2. "Satisfied that the **intruders** were gone, the wolverine ambled to a hidden storage spot, or cache."

CLUE: "The wolverine's instincts told it to either run away or stay hidden and be wary of these two-legged creatures."

   Ⓐ friends

   Ⓑ strangers

   Ⓒ bears

   Ⓓ houses

3. "The **repulsive** stench curbed the appetites of other scavengers, discouraging them from stealing the carcass."

CLUE: "Soon a half-eaten deer carcass was uncovered, reeking with a foul odor."

   Ⓐ pleasant

   Ⓑ red

   Ⓒ fresh

   Ⓓ disgusting

4. "Many people want laws to protect wolverines from being killed for their **pelts**."

CLUE: "Trappers consider the animal's fur valuable because the hairs repel ice crystals."

   Ⓐ eyes

   Ⓑ land

   Ⓒ skins

   Ⓓ tails

The Piranha: A Man-Eating Fish?

The movie scene opens like this: music warns you that something bad is going to happen. Loud drums beat a frantic rhythm. You see a man running through a lush green rain forest. High in the trees, birds and monkeys squawk at the disturbance below. The man's terror-filled eyes dart around. He glances over his shoulder while stumbling through the thick undergrowth. Sweat drips from his face and mingles with blood trickling from scratches on his skin. Why is he frightened? Is someone chasing him? Or maybe he's running from an animal.

[2]Suddenly, the man breaks out of the jungle. A river stretches before him. The music stops. With a look of relief, the man jumps into the water and swims toward the opposite riverbank. Halfway across, he slows down, then stops swimming. At once, his eyes widen in shock. Eerie, shrill music causes chills to sweep up your back as you watch the unfolding horror.

[3]"Help, help!" the man screams, thrashing wildly. He's being attacked! The water churns with dozens of fish. The fish are not large, but there are so many of them! Sharp teeth flash, tearing away chunks of flesh from the man's body. More fish join the horrific feeding frenzy. The river water turns red with blood that encircles the screeching man. He sinks beneath the water. Again, the music stops. Splashes slowly subside, and the fish disappear. It is strangely quiet. The camera zooms in on a swirl in the water. Rising, floating in the water is something white—a human skeleton! The vicious fish devoured the victim in only a few minutes.

[4]This is the typical way piranhas are portrayed in scary movies. Although much smaller than sharks, piranhas share the same people-killing, ruthless reputation. And, like

sharks, piranhas are among the most feared fish in the world.

[5]What's the real story? Is this not-so-big fish (average length: about 12 inches) as fearsome as its fame? How can a creature this size terrorize us? Where does it live?

[6]Piranhas thrive in the warm waters of South America. They are freshwater fish, found in lakes, lagoons, and rivers. A favorite spot for piranhas is the 4,000-mile-long Amazon River.

[7]At first glance, a piranha looks like an average fish. But its killer reputation starts with the teeth. A piranha's upper and lower jaws are loaded with triangle-shaped, razor-sharp teeth. Like a bulldog's mouth, the lower jaw juts out farther than the upper jaw. A piranha doesn't chew. It simply bites off chunks of a victim's body and swallows the pieces whole.

[8]The powerful teeth slide together like scissors. Long before scissors were invented, people in South America used piranha jaws as a handy cutting tool.

[9]A flat, oval-shaped body helps the piranha zip through the water. Not only is it a fast swimmer, but it can quickly change directions. A piranha's skin has glands that make a slimelike coating on its body. The slime protects the piranha from disease and gives it more speed through the water.

[10]About 25 species of piranhas live in South America. A common kind is the red-bellied piranha. It's colorful, with a gold or silver back and a bright red belly. Like most species, it is armed with deadly teeth.

[11]Another common type is the fierce red-eyed piranha, which grows up to 18 inches long. The jaws of this black-bodied fish are strong enough to bite through a piece of wood.

[12]Scientists still do not know much about how piranhas reproduce. It's believed that females lay their eggs during the rainy season. They deposit the eggs on floating plants or in muddy nests. After the babies (called "fry") hatch, they hide among rocks and plants, eating insects and seeds. While little, the silvery-colored fry are in danger of becoming food for birds or bigger fish.

[13]When the survivors grow large enough, they swim out to join the adult piranhas. A few types stick to a vegetarian diet, gulping down seeds, nuts, and fruits that fall into the water. These piranhas have sharper snouts with less ferocious-looking mouths. But most piranhas are blunt-nosed predators.

[14]Meat-eating piranhas will devour frogs, crabs, birds, fish, reptiles, and small mammals. Sometimes piranhas clip just the toes or tails of swimming animals. And piranhas have a habit of nibbling the fins and tails of other fish. One kind of fish, the cichlid, outsmarts the toothy nibblers. Several cichlids form a circle. They face outward, keeping their tail fins pointed toward the center of the circle. The piranhas leave them alone.

[15]A piranha might hunt by hiding among plants. If prey comes near, the piranha attacks. When a group of fish swims by, the ambushing piranha grabs one fish so quickly that the others swim on, unaware that anything happened.

[16]Some piranhas prefer to hunt in "schools." A school is a group of about 20 to 40 fish. A scientist watched a school of piranhas hunting a group of other fish. He said, "I saw one of the piranhas swim in and scatter the group of prey. Then in a flash, each piranha attacked and killed an individual prey fish."

[17]The piranha, however, is not at the top of the food chain. It has enemies. The crocodilelike caiman likes to chomp piranhas. Another predator is South America's largest snake, the anaconda. This 20- to 30-foot snake swims well and sometimes dines on a piranha.

[18]Giant otters also eat piranhas. How does an otter avoid the sharp teeth? Cleverly. First, the otter takes a big bite out of the side of the fish. Using its front paws, the otter holds the dying piranha up out of the water. Then the otter bites off the piranha's entire head and spits out the jaws and teeth. Now the giant otter can calmly munch on the rest of the fish.

[19]What about piranhas' reputation of devouring large animals and people? The people along the Amazon River have learned to live with piranhas. They swim in the same waters. Normally, piranhas do not bother healthy large animals or people. But if an animal or human happens to be bleeding, watch out!

[20]Four nostrils give the piranha an excellent sense of smell. A few drops of blood in the water can draw a crowd of hungry piranhas. This is the time when the fish are the most dangerous. The first piranhas to arrive at the bleeding animal begin biting. More blood flows. This excites the fish. Faster and faster, they violently strike the victim with knifelike teeth. A feeding frenzy develops when more piranhas

Can You Believe This?

join the attack. It's not a pretty sight.

[21]Amazonians use common sense and stay out of the water when aggressive piranhas are feeding on an animal. And during the dry season, people are especially careful. They do not wade or swim in drying-up lagoons or other small pools of water where food has become scarce for the trapped fish. At this time, starving piranhas will attack anything that enters the water. In the shrinking lakes and streams, they often become desperate enough to eat one another.

[22]When a person is bitten by a piranha, it's usually during a fishing accident. Piranhas are considered a tasty food source for Amazonians, so fishing for them is common. When a piranha is hooked and pulled out of the water, it is still alive. A blow to the piranha's head is needed. If it's not killed this way, its snapping jaws can claim a person's finger or toe.

[23]We know that piranhas can detect blood in the water. In addition, they sense underwater vibrations. Small hairs that grow in pores on their sides pick up slight movements. If an injured or sick animal struggles in the water, a school of piranhas might zero in and eliminate the animal.

[24]Some groups of Amazonians use the piranhas as "undertakers." During the rainy season when the land is flooded, it's difficult to bury dead people. Sometimes, a body is put into the water with piranhas. After a few hours, only a skeleton is left. It is retrieved, and the bones are dried. Later, the bones are buried when the floods are gone.

[25]It has been a challenge for researchers to study piranhas in their natural habitat. The waters where the fish live are filled with dangers. However, scientists have noted the importance of piranhas in the balance of nature.

[26]Most types of piranhas are considered to be scavengers, since they will eat dead animals. This is helpful. It stops the spread of diseases from rotting carcasses. Likewise, piranhas are useful when

they consume animals that are ill with contagious infections. Acting as nature's garbage disposal, piranhas keep the rain forest waters clean.

[27] Are piranhas vicious? Yes, they can be. Are they a threat to humans? No. They have more reasons to be afraid of us.

[28] Researchers will continue to teach us more about this fascinating fish. Like so many creatures that frighten us, our understanding of the piranha can turn our fear into respect.

If you have been timing your reading speed for this story, record your time below.

_____ : _____

Minutes   *Seconds*

UNDERSTANDING THE MAIN IDEA

The following questions will demonstrate your understanding of what the story is about, or the *main idea*. Choose the best answer for each question.

1. This story is mainly about

Ⓐ piranhas that eat people.

Ⓑ the habits of piranhas.

Ⓒ the caimans that eat piranhas.

Ⓓ how to swim safely among piranhas.

2. This story could have been titled

Ⓐ "Stay Out of the Water!"

Ⓑ "The Piranha's Bad Rap."

Ⓒ "Famous Piranha Movies."

Ⓓ "Feeding Frenzy."

3. Which detail best supports the main idea of the story?

Ⓐ With a look of relief, the man jumps into the river and starts to swim.

Ⓑ High in the trees, birds and monkeys squawk at the disturbance below.

Ⓒ A school is a group of about 20 to 40 fish.

Ⓓ Piranhas have more reason to be afraid of us than we do of them.

4. Find another detail that supports the main idea of this story. Write it on the lines below.

_____

_____

RECALLING FACTS

The following questions will test how well you remember the facts in the story you just read. Choose the best answer for each question.

1. Piranhas are

Ⓐ among the most feared fish in the world.

Ⓑ scarier than sharks and whales.

Ⓒ usually considered harmless.

Ⓓ known as vegetarians.

2. A favorite spot for piranhas is

Ⓐ the Arctic Circle.

Ⓑ the Amazon River.

Ⓒ the Nile.

Ⓓ the rivers of China.

3. People in South America used piranha jaws as

Ⓐ food.

Ⓑ hammers.

Ⓒ medicine.

Ⓓ scissors.

4. The piranha might be eaten by

Ⓐ monkeys.

Ⓑ smaller fish.

Ⓒ the anaconda snake.

Ⓓ meat-eating jungle plants.

READING BETWEEN THE LINES

An *inference* is a conclusion drawn from facts. A *generalization* is a general statement, idea, or rule that is supported by facts. Analyze the story by choosing the best answer to each question below.

1. What conclusion can you draw from paragraph 12?

Ⓐ Many baby piranhas are eaten.

Ⓑ Baby piranhas eat birds and other fish.

Ⓒ The mother piranhas protect their babies from predators.

Ⓓ It takes several months for piranha eggs to hatch.

2. What conclusion can you draw from paragraph 14?

Ⓐ Vegetarian piranhas often turn into meat-eaters.

Ⓑ Piranhas are very low swimmers.

Ⓒ Most of what piranhas eat are small animals.

Ⓓ Piranhas are not very intelligent.

3. What generalization can you make from the story?

Ⓐ Most of the time, piranhas are not a threat to humans.

Ⓑ All humans are in danger from piranhas.

Ⓒ Piranhas are the most vicious creatures alive.

Ⓓ Some piranhas eat only humans.

4. It can be inferred from the story that piranhas

Ⓐ are feared by all animals.

Ⓑ often don't eat bones.

Ⓒ would make wonderful pets.

Ⓓ are rapidly multiplying in North America.

Can You Believe This?

DETERMINING CAUSE AND EFFECT

Choose the best answers for the following questions to show the relationship between what happened in the story (*effects*) and why those things happened (*causes*).

1. Because piranhas' glands make a slimelike coating on their body, piranhas

Ⓐ are considered a delicacy in many countries.

Ⓑ leave a trail behind them in the water.

Ⓒ are protected from disease.

Ⓓ cannot be eaten.

2. What happens because piranhas often nibble the tails and fins of other fish?

Ⓐ Many fish drown when they become unable to swim.

Ⓑ Piranhas often starve to death.

Ⓒ Many veterinarians learn how to heal fish in the Amazon.

Ⓓ One kind of fish forms a group circle so piranhas can't reach their tails.

3. Why does the piranha have an excellent sense of smell?

Ⓐ Water conducts scent easily.

Ⓑ It can't see very well.

Ⓒ It has four nostrils.

Ⓓ Fish often have a strong odor.

4. Why is it hard to study piranhas in their natural habitat?

Ⓐ The waters where they live are very dangerous.

Ⓑ Piranhas are scared of people.

Ⓒ Amazonians try to keep piranhas a secret.

Ⓓ Piranhas move several thousand miles each year.

———■———

USING CONTEXT CLUES

Skilled readers often find the meaning of unfamiliar words by using *context clues*. This means they study the way the words are used in the text. Use the context clues in the excerpts below to determine the meaning of each **bold-faced** word. Then choose the answer that best matches the meaning of the word.

1. "The water **churns** with dozens of fish."

CLUE: "The fish are not large, but there are so many of them!"

- Ⓐ calms
- Ⓑ drains
- Ⓒ bubbles
- Ⓓ dries

2. "When a group of fish swims by, the **ambushing** piranha grabs one fish so quickly that the others swim on, unaware that anything happened." (paragraph 15)

Write what you think the **bold-faced** word means. Then record the context clues that led you to this definition.

Meaning:

_____

_____

_____

Context clues:

_____

_____

_____

3. "A **blow** to the piranha's head is needed."

CLUE: "If it's not killed this way, its snapping jaws can claim a person's finger or toe."

- Ⓐ puff of air
- Ⓑ hit
- Ⓒ gum
- Ⓓ kiss

4. "It has been a challenge for researchers to study piranhas in their natural **habitat**."

CLUE: "The waters where the fish live are filled with dangers."

- Ⓐ home
- Ⓑ dress
- Ⓒ nest
- Ⓓ eggs

——— ▬ ———

Can You Believe This?

End-of-Unit Activities

1. The title of this unit is "Freaks of Nature." The unit focused on only four oddities found in the natural world, but many more exist. Think of another "freak of nature." Then compare it to one of the "freaks of nature" in this unit. Use the Venn diagram below to display your comparisons and contrasts. List at least five similarities in the section where the circles overlap. List at least five differences in the individual circles. Make sure you label each circle.

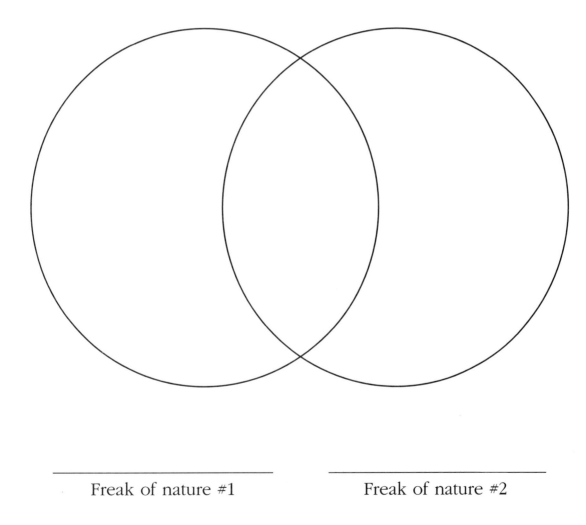

Freak of nature #1   Freak of nature #2

End-of-Unit Activities

2. **Rank each of the stories in this unit, from the one you liked the most to the one you liked the least. For each story, write one interesting fact you learned. Then write a paragraph describing why you liked the story you ranked *1* the best.**

LESSON 9 Ranking _____

_____

_____

_____

LESSON 10 Ranking _____

_____

_____

_____

LESSON 11 Ranking _____

_____

_____

_____

LESSON 12 Ranking _____

_____

_____

_____

Why did you like the story you ranked *1* the best?

_____

_____

_____

_____

_____

_____

Can You Believe This?

Words-Per-Minute Chart

UNIT THREE

Directions:

Use the chart to find your words-per-minute reading speed. Refer to the reading time you recorded at the end of each article. Find your reading time in seconds along the left-hand side of the chart or minutes and seconds along the right-hand side of the chart. Your words-per-minute score will be listed next to the time in the column below the appropriate lesson number.

No. of Words	Lesson 9 1127	Lesson 10 1286	Lesson 11 1386	Lesson 12 1496	
80	845	965	1040	1122	1:20
100	676	772	832	898	1:40
120	564	643	693	748	2:00
140	483	551	594	641	2:20
160	423	482	520	561	2:40
180	376	429	462	499	3:00
200	338	386	416	449	3:20
220	307	351	378	408	3:40
240	282	322	347	374	4:00
260	260	297	320	345	4:20
280	242	276	297	321	4:40
300	225	257	277	299	5:00
320	211	241	260	281	5:20
340	199	227	245	264	5:40
360	188	214	231	249	6:00
380	178	203	219	236	6:20
400	169	193	208	224	6:40
420	161	184	198	214	7:00
440	154	175	189	204	7:20
460	147	168	181	195	7:40
480	141	161	173	187	8:00
500	135	154	166	180	8:20
520	130	148	160	173	8:40
540	125	143	154	166	9:00
560	121	138	149	160	9:20
580	117	133	143	155	9:40
600	113	129	139	150	10:00
620	109	124	134	145	10:20
640	106	121	130	140	10:40
660	102	117	126	136	11:00
680	99	113	122	132	11:20
700	97	110	119	128	11:40
720	94	107	116	125	12:00
740	91	104	112	121	12:20
760	89	102	109	118	12:40
780	87	99	107	115	13:00
800	85	96	104	112	13:20
820	82	94	101	109	13:40
840	81	92	99	107	14:00

Seconds

Minutes and Seconds